THE PREPARED INTERN

Land Internships and Launch Your Career
by Knowing What Employers *Actually* Expect

LINDSAY MUENCH

with contributions from Susan Richardson

Table of Contents

Dedication

For my husband, whose unwavering support makes
everything possible.

For my children, who inspire me to grow and become
better every day.

For my mom, who always believes in me and helped
make this book a reality.

Introduction

I never planned to write a book. But that changed after my husband was injured flying an F-15 fighter jet, abruptly ending his Air Force career. Suddenly, he had to start over. He chose business school and set his sights on investment banking. But here's the catch: he had no finance experience, no interview experience beyond his high school job at Best Buy, and no idea how to navigate corporate America.

I spent more than a decade working in corporate America, so when he began preparing for this transition, I wanted to help.

I never relied on being the smartest or most qualified when pursuing internships or job opportunities. Instead, I relied on making sure I was always the most prepared. Every single time I've interviewed (seven times in total), I've walked away with an offer.

Of course, I checked the usual interview preparation boxes: a qualified résumé, tailoring my experience to the job requirements, researching the company and interviewers, and preparing thoughtful questions.

But there's another layer of preparation that most people skip, and that's what made the difference. I showed up prepared by simply knowing what employers evaluate *beyond* résumés and interview answers—the unspoken qualifications that rarely appear in job descriptions.

This is the part students usually overlook because it feels like "the easy stuff": how you show up, how you connect with others, how you carry yourself, and how you follow up. Yet these things are often the deciding factor between a rejection and an offer.

Once you've proven you're qualified on paper, hiring managers shift their focus to deciding if they like you as much as they like your résumé. They're asking themselves things like:

- *Can I see myself working with this person day-to-day?*
- *Will they earn the trust and respect of the team? Would they know how to act in a meeting?*
- *Would they represent our company well? Could I see them having lunch with a client?*

If the answer to any of those is no, it doesn't matter how impressive your résumé is; you probably won't get the offer. The hardest part is that most of the time, you won't be told the *real* reason you didn't get the offer, so you will continue to make the same mistakes. It's easy for a hiring manager to say, "We offered the role to someone else," but it's hard for them to say, "You didn't get the offer because it was difficult to have small talk with you, and you didn't make enough eye contact, so we can't imagine putting you in front of clients."

I had an advantage I didn't appreciate until college: my mom was a business etiquette trainer. At the time, it just meant I wrote more thank-you notes, had better dining skills, and shook hands more confidently than the average 18-year-old.

But when I started pursuing internships, it clicked. The lessons my mom taught me from a young age, such as making a good first impression, body language, presence, communication skills, and follow-up, turned out to be exactly what hiring managers actually wanted. That realization changed how I showed up, and it became an advantage that helped set me apart from others.

So when I was helping my husband, I didn't fix his résumé or run mock interviews with him. I focused on building his confidence by teaching him what to expect and what was expected of him. That way, even without the most qualified résumé, he was still seen as a strong candidate.

His preparation paid off. He landed the internship he wanted. Then the return offer.

That's when it hit me: If a driven, disciplined, and smart 30-something needed help figuring out how to navigate the expectations of the professional world after the military, what about the students just starting to think about their careers?

You've grown up connected through screens more than handshakes.

Your conversations often start with texts or DMs, not eye contact or phone calls.

Crucial years of your life were shaped by lockdowns, masks, and social distancing.

None of that is your fault. But here's the challenge: the world you grew up in changed, but the education system and the expectations of the workplace didn't. Many schools don't teach what's *actually* expected in the workplace, and many employers don't understand why the younger generation thinks and acts the way they do. That gap leaves many students stuck.

You cannot control how well school prepares you or the long-standing expectations employers still have, but you *can* give yourself a major advantage by learning how to bridge that gap. I wrote *The Prepared Intern* so you don't have to figure it all out on your own. It becomes much easier to show up prepared when you know what you are *actually* being evaluated on beyond your qualifications. Knowing these unspoken expectations can quickly elevate a candidate with basic qualifications or, just as quickly, sink someone highly qualified.

The Prepared Intern will help you turn networking into interviews, interviews into internship offers, and internships into full-time return offers. Paid internships make the time and money you invest in college pay off. According to a 2024 study, on average, paid interns received more job offers before graduation, as well as higher starting salaries (about $12,000-$15,000 higher!) than those with unpaid internships or no internship experience at all.[1]

I wrote *The Prepared Intern* with the person who taught me so much in the first place—my mom, Susan Richardson, a retired corporate business etiquette trainer who spent her career teaching Fortune 500 executives, business professionals, and college students.

This book is personal.

It's practical.

And it's built to help you not only land an internship, but launch a career.

---

[1] Kevin Gray, "Students Recognize the Importance of Gaining Internship Experience," NACE, September 23, 2024, https://naceweb.org/job-market/internships/students-recognize-the-importance-of-gaining-internship-experience.

Because graduating is the plan, but getting hired is the goal.

Before we dive in, let's define what it really means to be a *prepared intern.*

Rules are the baseline standards. Rules keep you out of trouble. Following them = *compliance.*

Expectations are the unspoken standards. Expectations create opportunities to stand out. Meeting (and exceeding) them = *credibility.*

Being prepared means showing up with the knowledge, skills, mindset, and behaviors that not only follow the *rules* but consistently meet and exceed the *expectations* employers value most.

And here's the best part: once your résumé (or network) gets you the interview, landing the offer isn't about being the smartest in the room; it's about being the most prepared. And preparation is one factor that's fully in your control. This is not about changing who you are. It's about learning how to present your best self.

Note: This book covers best practices. If your potential employer or current employer has alternative guidelines, please adhere to those. Keep in mind that every company has its own unique set of unspoken expectations, such as negative feelings toward those who don't attend company social events, or not promoting someone who doesn't dress the part. These are rarely written down, so it's important to be observant.

Before you go any further, please take two minutes to complete **The Prepared Intern Readiness Assessment**. This will give you a personalized snapshot of how prepared you are today and highlight the sections in this book that will help you the most.

Scan the QR code to get your results.
No email required.

The Unspoken Expectations of Professionalism: How to Be the Person People Want to Work With

Professionalism might sound boring, stuffy, or old-school, but it's the foundation of how people perceive you in work-related settings. Professionalism is the combination of habits, actions, and behaviors that make people trust you, respect you, and want to work with you.

Whether it's the person deciding who gets the internship, someone who could refer you to your dream job, or a future manager shaping your career path, how you show up and present yourself matters more than you think. That's why this topic comes first.

If you skip over the fundamentals like first impressions, body language, presence, and appearance, everything else you do (networking, interviewing, even your performance during an internship) risks being overshadowed. These fundamentals are often brushed off as "common sense," which is precisely why most people ignore them. Don't make that mistake.

Professionalism is rarely taught in school, but it's always noticed.

Learn it. Practice it. And most importantly, use it to your advantage.

First Impressions: Make Them Count

A first impression is the immediate opinion or feeling someone forms about you within the first few seconds of meeting you. They're making an assumption about you based on what they see (your appearance, your body language, your facial expressions), not what they can't see (your personality, your experience, your intelligence). It is your responsibility to utilize a first impression to your advantage by being aware of what is being assessed.

- 55% is based on your body language and appearance (not what you look like, but how you present yourself)
- 38% is your tone (how you say it)
- Only 7% of it are the actual words you say

This research, conducted by psychologist Albert Mehrabian, reveals that nonverbal signals carry more weight than words when someone is forming an opinion of you.[2]

What's Actually Happening When a First Impression Is Made

1. People form opinions in 7 to 15 seconds.
2. After an opinion is quickly formed, they subconsciously look for proof that supports their opinion.
3. They seek out, interpret, and remember information that confirms their initial judgment of you, while ignoring or discounting information that contradicts it. This bias makes first impressions especially powerful.

---

[2] Albert Mehrabian, *Silent Messages*, 1971, Wadsworth Publishing Co.

Why This Matters

If you make a strong first impression (e.g., you appear confident and likeable during an introduction), others are more likely to notice behaviors that reinforce that positive view, overlook mistakes or awkwardness that contradict it, and give you the benefit of the doubt in uncertain situations.

The reverse is also true. A weak or awkward first impression may cause others to focus on flaws or missteps, attribute neutral behavior negatively, and be less open to changing their judgment, even after positive interactions.

Pro Tip: From the moment you walk in, *everyone* you interact with is subconsciously sizing you up. Make sure you're sending the right signals to prompt a yes to these questions decision-makers are asking themselves:

- *Can I see myself working with this person every day?*
- *Will they earn the trust and respect of the team?*
- *Would they represent our company well?*

What People Notice First

- Eye contact
- Your smile
- Handshake
- How you introduce yourself
- Posture
- Appearance
- Overall energy

Tips for Making a Strong First Impression

- Always be aware of both your verbal and nonverbal actions (especially eye contact!).

- The quickest way to break the ice, appear approachable, and make someone feel comfortable and at ease during an introduction is to smile.

- Remember that it's easier to make a good first impression than to correct a bad one.

Pro Tip: Be mindful of the quickest ways to ruin a first impression (especially in an interview): avoiding eye contact, being dressed inappropriately, slouching in a chair, and using slang language, poor grammar, or swear words.

Body Language and Nonverbal Communication: What You Say Without Speaking

People form opinions before you even speak, and your body language immediately reveals three things: Whether you are paying attention, whether you are showing respect, and whether you are putting in effort and genuinely care.

Body Language Tips

- Eyes show interest, a smile breaks the ice and builds a connection, and good posture shows confidence.

- Be more aware of your actions in professional settings. For example, it might seem obvious not to roll your eyes or slouch in a chair, but these actions may happen out of habit, so be extra cautious.

From my experience, these are some of the worst habits that drive people crazy: yawning during a conversation without covering your mouth, twirling your hair, picking a scab, biting your nails, and clicking a pen. Habits are hard to break, but being aware of them is half the battle.

- Keep your hands away from your mouth when you are speaking.

- Respect personal space. Standing too close makes others feel uncomfortable. The recommended distance for business settings is about two to three feet to ensure comfort.

- When there is a contradiction between what you are saying and what you are doing, actions speak louder than words. For example, if you are talking to a recruiter and say, "I'm really interested in interviewing with your company," but you're looking at your phone, your words will be disregarded.

- To connect and encourage conversation with someone while standing, position your body so both your shoulders and your feet are facing them.

- Learn to observe, read, and understand the body language of others. This skill will give you an advantage when interacting with people both personally and professionally.

Eye Contact

Why It Matters

Eye contact is a powerful nonverbal skill that communicates interest, builds trust, and helps establish rapport. When you look away while speaking, your words can lose their impact and seem less convincing.

In fact, 68% of employers identify a lack of eye contact as the most common nonverbal mistake, and 65% of interviewers admit they have chosen not to hire candidates who failed to maintain appropriate eye contact.[3] Maintaining steady, confident eye contact can make a significant difference in how your message is received and how you are perceived.

Tips to Improve

- Be aware of the importance of eye contact.
- Practice eye contact in low-pressure situations. The next time you're ordering food or checking out at a store, look the person in the eye long enough to notice their eye color and say, "Thank you."
- Keep in mind, there's a difference between a hard stare and respectful eye contact.

Facial Expressions

Why It Matters

According to a CareerBuilder survey, more than one-third of hiring managers reported that seeing candidates not smile is a common nonverbal mistake during interviews.[4]

---

[3] Written by Andrei Kurtuy Co-Founder & Career Expert Andrei combines academic knowledge with over 10 years of practical experience to help job seekers navigate the challenges of résumés et al., "75+ Job Interview Statistics That Will Help You Get Hired in 2025," Novoresume, September 15, 2025, https://novoresume.com/career-blog/job-interview-statistics.

[4] Martha C. White, "Bad Body Language Is Common in Job Interviews," Time, February 9, 2015, https://time.com/3700018/how-you-could-botch-a-job-interview-without-saying-a-word.

Tips to Improve

- If smiling doesn't come naturally, focus on doing it during certain moments, such as greeting someone, when others smile at you, and when saying thank you.

- To appear engaged, keep your facial expression active and interested. Try raising your eyebrows slightly, nodding occasionally, or offering a small smile when someone is speaking to you. These subtle cues signal that you're attentive, curious, and genuinely interested in the conversation and will also help you avoid inadvertently having a blank stare.

Posture

Why It Matters

Even if you simply struggle with bad posture, remember that it's a form of nonverbal communication. The way you carry yourself shows everything from confidence to engagement to respect. Standing or sitting tall conveys confidence and presence, while slouching can suggest low energy, disinterest, or even a lack of professionalism.

Tips to Improve
Standing posture:

- Imagine a string lifting you from the top of your head.
- Relax and roll your shoulders back.
- Keep your feet shoulder-width apart with your weight evenly balanced.
- Keep your arms relaxed at your sides; avoid crossed arms.
- Avoid leaning against objects (walls, desks, etc.).

Sitting posture:

- Sit tall, ribcage lifted, shoulder blades back, and no slouching.
- Keep both feet flat on the floor with your knees at a 90-degree angle.
- Rest your hands on your lap, the table, or on armrests.
- Avoid leaning, slouching, or fidgeting (such as tapping, kicking your foot, or bouncing your knees).

Professional Presence: How You Show Up Matters

Professional presence is the combination of how you present yourself, communicate, and behave in ways that demonstrate confidence, maturity, and credibility in a professional setting.

5 Elements of Professional Presence

Professional presence is about being intentional and acting like you belong (even if you don't have it all figured out). When you take yourself seriously, others will too.

1. **Appearance**
   - This is *not* about what you look like. It's about showing up looking sharp, which means you're well-groomed, clean, and intentional. This also includes having good posture, making eye contact, and carrying yourself with confidence and purpose.
   - Dress in a way that shows you belong and that you respect the setting's standards for professionalism. It demonstrates that you take both the opportunity and the people around you seriously.

2. **Energy**
   - Be calm, engaged, and focused.
   - You should be attentive and show enthusiasm about the opportunity, as people want to hire those who are excited about the role and the company.

3. **Communication**
   - Speak clearly, no mumbling, and vary your tone to avoid sounding monotone.
   - Limit filler words like *um, uh,* and *like.*
   - Pay attention to both your verbal delivery and your nonverbal body language.

4. **Listening**
   - Maintain eye contact.
   - Practice active listening to show engagement (e.g., nod your head occasionally).
   - Avoid interrupting others.

5. **Responsiveness**
   - Reply to emails, calls, and texts promptly.
   - Follow up after interviews with a thank-you.

Common Professional Presence Mistakes

These are missteps you may not even realize you're making:

- Showing up late (or not early enough).
- Speaking too casually in professional settings.
- Not paying attention to your body language.

- Dressing too casually or not in line with the dress code.
- Checking your phone or watch during conversations out of habit.

How to Nail the Handshake: Small Gesture, Big Impact

- A handshake should always be firm, but not bone-crushing, regardless of whether you're shaking hands with a man or a woman.

- In formal business settings, handshakes are the standard for greetings and introductions. In casual environments, people may opt for alternatives such as a nod, a wave, a verbal greeting with a smile, or an elbow bump. It's best to follow the other person's lead.

- Always stand to meet or greet someone, especially when shaking hands.

- Initiate a handshake with confidence, making eye contact as you extend your right hand parallel with the ground, with your thumb up. Hands should meet web to web and palm to palm (not palm to fingers) with a firm (not crushing) grip.

- Shake with two to three pumps, about two to three seconds, while maintaining eye contact to show interest. At this time, also introduce yourself.

- Use the other person's name during or immediately after the handshake to help remember it.

- Carry drinks, notebooks, and other items in your left hand so your right is free to shake hands.

- Interviews start and end with a handshake.

Dress Codes: What to Wear (and Why It Matters)

Before you say a word, your appearance has already made an impression. Appearance is about how you present yourself, not what you look like. You may not like or agree with the dress code (and some of it might feel outdated or uncomfortable), but in professional settings, appearance and presentation matter and should be taken seriously.

Following the dress code shows respect. Just like you wouldn't show up to your friend's black tie wedding in jeans, you shouldn't show up to an interview with jeans if the dress code is business professional. Similar to first impressions, people will make assumptions based on how you show up, and those assumptions can either work for you or against you.

Dress for the Role You Want

Note: These are general recommendations. It is important to prioritize the dress code policies outlined by the employer if they are different from the suggestions below.

Tips to look your best:

- Always be well-groomed. At a minimum, this means being clean and neat.

- When in doubt, dress more conservatively and formally.

- Do not mistake casual clothes for *business* casual attire.

- Neatness is always more important when you are dressed casually.

- Be conscientious of the fit of your clothing. Proper fit and tailoring your clothing (if necessary) are more important than the cost or brand of the clothing.

- Dark colors complement your shape and create the appearance of authority.

- Avoid clothes that have stains, rips, holes, or missing buttons.

- Keep your clothing well-maintained and utilize dry cleaning as needed.

- Choose wrinkle-free options, such as performance materials, if you prefer not to iron.

- When buying a suit, do the "scrunch" test to test wrinkle resistance. The scrunch test is when you ball up the fabric with your hands to see if wrinkles are easily created.

- If you purchase a suit jacket or sport coat and there is thread to keep the jacket flaps in place in the back, cut it before wearing. The same is true with the back slit of a woman's skirt.

- Keep your shoes polished (if leather) and in excellent condition.

- Match your socks to your pants, not your shoes. Stick to solid or subtle patterns for interview settings. Socks should be high enough to cover your shin when sitting.

- Belts should match the color of your shoes.

- Pay attention to the condition of your accessories, such as a padfolio, pen, briefcase, purse, or umbrella.

- Your hands are very noticeable, so make sure you take care of your nails. This applies to both genders.

- Avoid chewing gum. It is not appropriate in business settings.

Men:

Business Professional

Suits in dark or neutral colors (e.g., navy or gray) with a long-sleeved dress shirt and tie (depending on scenario). Dress pants and a belt with a button-down shirt and a blazer or sport coat are also acceptable. Polished dress shoes with dress socks that match pants and minimal accessories.

Business Casual

Dress pants, chinos, or dark jeans paired with a collared shirt, such as a button-down or polo, which can also be worn under a quarter-zip, sweater, or blazer. Performance dress pants paired with loafers is also a popular choice. Don't forget a belt.

Tips:

- Regarding suit jacket buttons:
  - Two-Button Jacket
    - Top button: Buttoned when standing
    - Bottom button: Never buttoned
    - When sitting: Unbutton completely
  - Three-Button Jacket
    - Top button: Optional (can be buttoned or left undone)
    - Middle button: Always buttoned when standing
    - Bottom button: Never buttoned
    - When sitting: Unbutton completely

- Wear a long-sleeve shirt with a suit.
- Make sure your collar and sleeve lengths are sized correctly.
- Ties should be tied long enough to reach the tip of your belt buckle.
- Hair, facial hair, and nails should be well-groomed.
- Apply cologne and aftershave sparingly or not at all.
- When selecting dress shoes, know that the thinner the sole, the dressier the shoe.

Women:

Business Professional

Dresses, pant suits, or skirt suits with a blouse or top. Shoulders should be covered. Closed-toe heels, minimal jewelry, and neat hairstyles.

Business Casual:

Dress pants, dark jeans, skirts, or dresses paired with blouses, knit tops, or sweaters. Flats, loafers, or heels are common.

Tips:

- Avoid all clothing that is too revealing, including clothes that are too tight, too short, or that show cleavage.
- Jewelry, makeup, and hairstyle should be kept simple.
- Apply perfume and scented hand lotion sparingly.
- If you choose to paint your nails, select a color that is appropriate for your workplace environment.

Dry Cleaning Basics

Dry cleaning keeps dress clothes crisp, structured, and stain-free, which is essential for interviews, internships, and networking events.

What to Dry Clean

- Wool or wool-blended suits or blazers
- Dress shirts (especially if they stain or wrinkle easily)
- Silk, linen, or specialty fabrics
- Men's ties
- Clothes labeled "dry clean only"

Rule of thumb: If you'd wear it to an interview or formal event, treat it with extra care.

Pro Tips:

- Rotate your wardrobe and don't over-wash or over-dry-clean clothes, as this can wear them out.
- Use garment bags to protect clothes in transit and from closet dust. If it's something you don't wear often, avoid storing it in plastic garment bags because they can cause clothing to yellow by trapping moisture.
- When getting your cotton dress shirts dry-cleaned, ask for *light* starch for crispness without stiffness.

The Small Details Matter

Before interviews, networking events, or important first meetings, do a quick personal appearance check. These details may seem minor, but they can strongly influence the impression you make, especially in professional settings.

- Nails: Keep your nails clean and trimmed. If wearing polish, keep it neat and free from chips.
- Hair: Clean, brushed, and styled away from your face; facial hair (if any) trimmed and maintained.
- Hygiene: Fresh breath, deodorant, no overpowering fragrances
- Clothing: Clean, wrinkle-free, stain-free, and lint-free; properly fitted
- Jewelry: Simple and clean
- Makeup (if worn): Not distracting
- Socks: Match to your pants
- Belt: Match with the color of your shoes
- Shoes: Clean, polished (if leather), and in good condition

Accessories Matter Too

Even items that seem secondary say something about your professionalism:

- Phone case: Clean, simple, not flashy
- Notebook or padfolio: Presentable and organized
- Pen: Reliable, professional-looking (for example, do not bring a freebie pen with a company logo)
- Bag, backpack, or purse: Neutral, clean, and in good condition

Wrap-Up: The Unspoken Expectations of Professionalism

Being prepared means more than following the rules. It means knowing what's expected even when no one spells it out.

First Impressions

- Rule: Be polite when meeting someone new.
- Expectation: Arrive early. Make a confident entrance. Stand tall. Smile genuinely. Say your name with energy and make strong eye contact.

Body Language

- Rule: Be aware of your nonverbal communication.
- Expectation: Own the room without saying a word. Sit and stand with a posture that communicates confidence. Use facial expressions and eye contact to show you're engaged and self-aware.

Professional Presence

- Rule: Look and act like you belong.
- Expectation: Present yourself appropriately. Speak clearly, listen actively, and carry yourself with calm energy, focus, and maturity. Everything from your tone to your appearance should reflect readiness and respect.

Handshakes

- Rule: Shake hands when introduced.
- Expectation: Make your introduction count. Stand to greet, make eye contact, and offer a firm, confident handshake. Say their name to create connection, and show that you're fully present.

Dress Code

- Rule: Wear appropriate clothes.
- Expectation: Dress with intention. Well-fitted, well-maintained clothing, along with appropriate grooming, shows that you take yourself and the role seriously.

Final Takeaway:

How you show up tells people how seriously to take you. Look presentable, act engaged, and you'll earn respect before you even say a word. When you look good, you feel good, and that helps you show up as your best self.

The Unspoken Expectations of Professional Communication: Write, Speak, and Show Up Like You Belong

Communication skills consistently top the list of what employers want. In 2024, LinkedIn ranked communication as the #1 most in-demand skill.[5]

Strong communication skills start with mastering the basics. The way you talk to friends is not the same way you should speak to professors, recruiters, or hiring managers. It may sound obvious, but recognizing your audience and adjusting your style is a signal of maturity and preparedness for professional settings.

Personal Communication (Friends, peers)

- Fast, casual, often slang or emojis
- No formal greetings or sign-offs
- Impulsive or shorthand responses

Professional Communication (Co-workers, customers, teachers, mentors)

- Clear, structured, and purposeful

---

[5] "The Most In-Demand Skills of 2024," LinkedIn, accessed September 29, 2025, https://www.linkedin.com/business/talent/blog/talent-strategy/linkedin-most-in-demand-hard-and-soft-skills.

- Tone matches the situation (confident, respectful, and clear)
- Complete sentences, proper grammar, and no unnecessary slang

Example:

Personal: *"Hey, hit me up when you're free."*

Professional: *"Would you be available for a quick call this afternoon?"*

Quick Self-Check Before You Send or Say It

1. **Audience:** Who am I talking to: friend, teacher, recruiter?
2. **Tone:** Does this sound confident, respectful, and clear?
3. **Context:** What's the setting: email, interview, text?

Pro Tip: In most workplaces, communication starts out professional and can become casual over time. Don't skip that process. Earn trust and credibility first, which will naturally lead to building more personal rapport. Remember that some topics are *always* off-limits in a professional setting, even once you're friendly with colleagues. These include:

- Politics and religion
- Personal finances
- Gossip
- Romantic relationships
- Negative opinions about the company or boss

Verbal Communication: How to Sound Confident and Competent

Why It Matters

About 96% of employers list communication as the most important career readiness skill for recent graduates, yet only about 53% rate graduates as very or extremely proficient in that area.[6]

Verbal communication, in particular, reveals confidence, clarity, and maturity, or a lack thereof. In many situations, how you speak matters even more than what you say. If you don't sound like you believe in yourself, it's unlikely that others will believe in you either.

What Makes a Great Communicator:

- Speaks clearly and confidently
- Listens more, talks less
- Is polite ("Please," "Thank you," "Excuse me," "I appreciate your time")
- Puts others at ease
- Can talk about many different subjects
- Asks good and engaging questions
- Does not interrupt when others are talking
- Gives the other person their full, undivided attention
- Keeps their cell phone out of sight and muted or turned off
- Accepts compliments gracefully by just saying "thank you" and extends compliments with sincerity

[6] Kevin Gray, "The Gap in Perceptions of New Grads' Competency Proficiency and Resources to Shrink It," Default, January 13, 2025, https://www.naceweb.org/career-readiness/competencies/the-gap-in-perceptions-of-new-grads-competency-proficiency-and-resources-to-shrink-it.

- Knows when to talk business and when not to
- Reads body language

Tips to Improve:

- Focus on pacing. Talking too fast or too slow distracts from the words being said.
- Avoid slang and swearing.
- Eliminate filler words ("like," "um," "you know," "basically," "just") and upspeak (when your voice rises at the end of a sentence, even if you're not asking a question).
- Avoid certain topics when making small talk with new acquaintances, including politics, religion, sex, and gossip.
- In a conversation, when someone is talking, your intention should be to listen, show genuine interest, and refrain from thinking about your reply.
- Be careful not to interrupt others, as it can be perceived that you feel your thoughts are more important than their thoughts. If you have a habit of interrupting, try this trick: After someone finishes a sentence, count slowly to two (in your head), then begin talking.

Phone Calls

- The tone and clarity of your voice are more important than the words.
- It's extremely important to make sure you're enunciating clearly on the phone.
- Smile when you are on the phone. Your voice and your attitude will both sound better. Another tip to sound better while on the phone is to stand up when talking.

- Return calls as soon as possible (no longer than 24 hours).

- Never chew gum, eat, or drink while you are on the phone, as noise can be magnified.

- To best connect with the person you're speaking with, mirror their tone and energy. If they want to dive right into the conversation and skip small talk, follow their lead.

- When making a call, always begin by introducing yourself, your company (if applicable), and with whom you would like to speak.

- When you answer a call, start by saying "Hello" or "Hi, this is [First Name]" because it comes across as awkward and unprofessional if you stay silent and wait for the caller to speak first.

- When receiving a call, immediately write down the caller's name and use it sparingly throughout the conversation. This helps build rapport and connection.

- If you are disconnected during a conversation, it is the responsibility of the caller to place the call again.

- Keep your phone on silent mode, airplane mode, or powered off during interviews and meetings.

- If you are expecting a call during a meeting, it is best to let the meeting organizer know in advance.

- Excuse yourself quickly and quietly if you are in a meeting and need to answer a call.

- Alleviate phone tag by scheduling a specific day and time for a conversation.

Voicemails

- Always be prepared to leave a voicemail message.

- When leaving a message, information should be left in this order: your name, school or company name (if applicable), telephone number, message, and telephone number again.

- Be concise, enunciate, and do not talk too fast.

- Keep your voicemail greeting up to date. Here are a few examples:

  - "Hi, this is Lindsay Muench. I can't take your call right now, but please leave your name, number, and a brief message, and I'll get back to you as soon as I can."

  - "Hi, you've reached Lindsay Muench. Sorry I missed your call! Please leave your name, number, and a quick message, and I'll return your call as soon as I can."

- Your voicemail may be someone's first impression of you. Therefore, call your own telephone number and make sure your voicemail leaves the impression you want to make.

Small Talk: How to Be More Likeable and Less Awkward in Any Conversation

Small talk is casual, light conversation about noncontroversial topics, often used to break the ice, build rapport, or fill the silence in social or professional settings. Small talk is important because it builds relationships, shows your emotional intelligence, improves collaboration, and opens unexpected doors. Even if you don't like small talk just because you're shy, avoiding it is usually interpreted by others as a sign that you're not interested or that you're rude.

How to Be Good at Small Talk

Be friendly, smile, use open posture (avoid crossed arms or slouching), and maintain eye contact.

Build Rapport

- Show genuine curiosity.
- Ask one or two open-ended questions.
- Share something about yourself.
- Find common ground.

Practice Mindful Listening

- Stay present and focused.
- Avoid interrupting.
- Respond to what the other person says.

Read the Room

- Pay attention to body language and tone.
- If someone seems distracted or uninterested, exit the conversation gracefully.

Tips to Improve

Ask open-ended questions that start with how, what, or why:

- *"How do you know the host?"*
- *"What made you want to work at [company name]?"*
- *"Why did you choose to go to [school name]?"*

Use other conversation starters:

- Compliment: *"You're doing a great job on that project. What's been your favorite part?"*

- Shared moment: *"What was your favorite part of that presentation?"*

- Commonality: *"I'm from Wisconsin too. What city did you grow up in?"*

Pro Tip: Practice small talk to help build confidence. Take advantage of everyday, low-pressure situations, such as waiting in line, talking to servers, talking to receptionists, etc.

Introductions and Elevator Pitches: Make Yourself Memorable

A great introduction builds trust and credibility. Even if you're lacking experience, a strong introduction can make a difference. It sets the tone for the conversation.

When Introducing Yourself

- Say your full name confidently:

  "Hi, I'm Jordan Lee."

- Add quick context:

  "I'm a freshman at Villanova, interested in sales internships."

- Eye contact, a smile, and good energy make all the difference.

When Introducing Others

- If you do not know the correct pronunciation of someone's name, ask.

- Provide context or information about the individuals you are introducing.
- Always remember to make introductions before jumping into a conversation.

Remembering Names

- Hear it, say it in your head, repeat it, and then use it sparingly in the conversation. *"It's nice to meet you, Ann." "Goodbye, Ann."*
- Pay attention to the person's name to make sure you really hear it so you can pronounce it correctly and remember it.
- Make a connection with the name you hear to someone else you know who has the same name. My trick is that when I meet someone new, I associate them with someone I know. For instance, if I met someone named Billy, I would associate them with my cousin named Billy. Then, when I see Billy next, I will think of my cousin and be able to quickly remember his name.
- Write the name down, especially if you are seated in a meeting or an interview and then use it occasionally.
- If you have forgotten someone's name, be honest, and, with sincerity in your voice, admit it and ask them to please remind you what it is.

Building Your Elevator Pitch

An elevator pitch is a short summary of who you are, what you do, and what you're looking for delivered in the time it takes to ride an elevator (usually 30 seconds to two minutes). The goal is to quickly build interest, establish credibility, and open the door for further conversation.

30-Second Elevator Pitch

- **Purpose:** Quick introduction, spark curiosity, leave the listener wanting to know more
- **Structure:**
  1. Who you are
  2. What you do/your value
  3. What you're seeking or your "ask"
- **Tone:** Concise, energetic, and memorable
- **Best For:** Networking events, career fairs, or unplanned introductions

Examples:

"Hi, I'm Alex Chen, a sophomore at Wake Forest majoring in finance. I've been exploring investment banking and recently completed a finance bootcamp to build my modeling skills. I'm hoping to learn more about how professionals like you got started in the field."

"Hi, I'm Mia Johnson, a sophomore at the University of Tennessee, majoring in supply chain management. I've been helping my family's small business improve inventory processes, and I'm really interested in logistics. I'd love to learn more about how supply chain careers work in larger companies."

"Hi, I'm Ava Thompson, a sophomore at Elon majoring in marketing. I've been managing my sorority's recruitment content and interning with a local startup on social media

strategy. I'm excited to learn more about careers in brand marketing and how professionals broke into the industry."

Two-Minute Elevator Pitch

- **Purpose:** A more complete introduction that allows you to tell a bit more of your story, highlight key accomplishments, and connect your background to your audience.

- **Structure:**
  1. Who you are
  2. Brief background (education, experience)
  3. Key transferable/applicable skills or achievements
  4. What you're looking for and why you're interested
  5. Engage with a question or invitation to talk further

- **Tone:** Still concise but with enough detail to build rapport and credibility.

- **Best For:** Interviews ("Tell me about yourself"), informational meetings, networking coffee chats, or planned professional introductions.

Here are a few examples:
Example 1:

Who you are:

"Hi, I'm Alex Chen. I'm currently a sophomore at Wake Forest University, majoring in finance."

Brief background (education, experience):

"Over the past year, I've been exploring the world of finance, especially investment banking. I took part in a virtual finance boot camp, where I learned the fundamentals of financial modeling, valuation

techniques, and Excel best practices. That experience really sparked my interest in the strategic side of business transactions."

Key skills or achievements:

"In addition to the bootcamp, I've been building my skillset by participating in our university's student investment fund, where I helped analyze and pitch equities for our portfolio. I've also connected with a few alumni in the finance space to better understand the day-to-day work and career paths in the industry."

What you're looking for and why you're interested:

"Right now, I'm looking for opportunities to gain hands-on exposure through a summer internship, ideally in a fast-paced, deal-oriented environment. I'm drawn to investment banking because I enjoy solving complex problems under pressure and collaborating with driven teams. I also appreciate the steep learning curve and the opportunity to learn how businesses are valued and positioned for growth."

Engage with a question or invitation to talk further:

"I'd love to hear more about your own journey, especially how you got started and what you wish you knew as a student trying to break in. Would you be open to sharing a bit about your path or any advice for someone exploring this field?"

Example 2:

Who you are:

"Hi, I'm Mia Johnson, a sophomore at the University of Tennessee, majoring in supply chain management."

Brief background (education, experience):

"I come from a family of small business owners, so I've grown up watching the challenges of inventory, shipping, and customer satisfaction firsthand. Recently, I've been helping my family improve their order tracking and vendor coordination, which sparked a deeper interest in logistics and operational efficiency."

Key skills or achievements:

"That hands-on experience, combined with what I've learned in my supply chain coursework, has helped me build a practical understanding of concepts such as lead time, demand forecasting, and warehouse layout. I've also taken the initiative to get more technical by learning Excel-based inventory models. I am starting to explore tools like Power BI and Tableau to visualize data and improve decision-making."

What you're looking for and why you're interested:

"I'm currently seeking internship opportunities where I can apply these skills in a larger-scale environment, ideally within a company that values process improvement and data-driven decision-making. I'm excited about supply chain because it's fast-moving, essential, and full of opportunities for innovation."

Engage with a question or invitation to talk further:

"I'd love to hear how you first got into the supply chain field and what skills you think are most valuable for someone trying to stand out early in their career. Would you be open to sharing your story?"

Example 3:

Who you are:

"Hi, I'm Ava Thompson, a sophomore at Elon, where I'm majoring in marketing with a focus on digital strategy."

Brief background (education, experience):

"I've always been drawn to storytelling and brand building, so I've sought out opportunities where I can blend creativity with strategy. This year, I've been managing my sorority's recruitment content by planning campaigns, filming reels, and tracking engagement. I've also been interning with a local startup where I support their social media and email marketing efforts."

Key skills or achievements:

"Through those roles, I've gotten hands-on experience with Canva, Meta Business Suite, and Mailchimp, and I've learned how to build and adapt content based on analytics and feedback. I've also worked closely with the startup's founder, which gave me a front-row seat to how brand consistency and user experience play a role in early growth. That experience made me even more excited to explore brand strategy at scale."

What you're looking for and why you're interested:

"Right now, I'm looking to learn from professionals who are doing this work at the next level, whether that's in-house brand teams, marketing agencies, or consumer product companies. I love the challenge of connecting with an audience and shaping perception, and I'm eager to better understand the business side of creative marketing."

Engage with a question or invitation to talk further:

"I'd love to hear how your team approaches brand storytelling, particularly how you strike a balance between creativity and performance

metrics. Does the internship program give exposure to that kind of strategic thinking?"

Pro Tips:

- Don't memorize word-for-word so that it's conversational, yet polished.

- Smile and speak with energy.

- Tailor it to the situation (especially at the beginning of interviews).

- End with a question or next step, such as: "… and I'd love to hear how you got started in that field."

- Write out both your short and long elevator pitches so you have them as go-to templates that can easily be adapted depending on the audience or situation.

Digital Communication: Write Like You're More Experienced Than You Are

Whether it's texting, emailing, or calling, how you communicate = how you're perceived.

Texting

- Keep your tone professional and your message clear and concise.

- Avoid using slang, overly casual language, or emojis, as they can diminish the professionalism of your message.

- Regarding emojis—use them sparingly and only use them if the person you're communicating with uses them first. Only use emojis if you know your recipient well enough to gauge their acceptance of them, and make sure that the emoji matches the context and can't be misunderstood.

- Send work-related texts or direct messages only during working hours unless there is an emergency or a prior understanding with the recipient. Late-night or early-morning texts and direct messages can be seen as intrusive.

- Be mindful of different time zones if working with recruiters in other parts of the country, remote teams, or clients abroad.

- Always proofread your message to avoid embarrassing mistakes or misunderstandings due to autocorrect. Business communication, even over text or direct message, should reflect attention to detail.

- Avoid abbreviations like "u" for "you" or "thx" for "thanks." These can come across as too casual and unprofessional.

- When sending someone a text for the first time, include your name and a brief context.

- Avoid sending sensitive or confidential information over text or direct message, as it may not be as secure as other communication methods.

- Be mindful of group messages; ensure they are relevant to all participants, and respect people's time by keeping them brief.

- Don't expect immediate replies and avoid sending follow-up texts or direct messages too soon. Allow the recipient some time to respond, especially outside regular working hours.

- When someone replies to your text or direct message, acknowledge their response to close the loop, even if just with a "Thanks for your input."

Email

- Email is never anonymous, and you have no control over what may be forwarded. With that being said, always get consent before forwarding an email.

- When reaching out to a potential employer, use a professional email address or your school email address.

  Good example: firstname.lastname@email.com

  Bad example: hotsoccergirl@gmail.com

- Do not treat email like text messages because it is considered a more formal form of communication.

- Your greeting should be polite, formal, and personalized to the recipient, especially when reaching out for the first time. "Dear [Name]" is the most appropriate greeting. A more casual yet often acceptable greeting is "Hi [Name]." If there is an ongoing email thread, you do not need to include the greeting every time.

- Avoid typing in all capital letters because it can come across as shouting. However, do use standard capitalization rules, such as capitalizing the first word of each sentence and proper nouns. These details are often overlooked in casual text messages.

- Break up large blocks of text into short paragraphs for readability and use bullet points as needed. If the email becomes too lengthy, it may be appropriate to schedule a call instead.

- Always fill out the subject line to ensure your email is read; this should also make it clear why you're reaching out.

- Use the "out of office" response feature.

- Include the following in your signature block: full name, university and graduation year, email address, LinkedIn profile link, and phone number (optional). If you have an email address through a company (during an internship, etc.), you will likely have a standardized company signature block, and you should abide by that format.

  John Smith
  ABC University | Class of 2028
  john.smith@abcuniversity.edu
  linkedin.com/in/johnsmith

- Remember, an email is a reflection of your professionalism and the company that you represent. Proofread for typos. Use Grammarly (if needed) and reread your email before hitting send.

- If you're including attachments, attach them before writing the email so you don't forget to include them. Make sure the file name is appropriate and clear.

- Be very careful sending humorous material or any material that could be interpreted as offensive. Again, you are a reflection of your company, not just yourself.

- Respond to emails promptly, within 24 hours, even if it is to acknowledge that you have received it. In some industries, 24 hours may be too slow, so make sure to know the expectations of your company and industry.

- The recruiter or client, not you, determines a preferred method of communication such as texting, calling, or email.

- Look at the signature at the end of an email for your contact's name preference (Mike vs. Michael).

- Use a professional closing. "Best regards" is a safe choice.

- To alleviate an email being sent prematurely, wait until after you have finished the content of the message and have proofread it before you enter the recipient's email address.

- When responding to an email with multiple recipients, carefully choose between "Reply" and "Reply All" to ensure your message reaches only the people who need it.

- Avoid sending emails that have no clear ask or purpose.

- When emailing someone for the first time, default to a formal greeting (e.g., "Ms. Richardson" or "Dr. Snider"). For coworkers and peers, first names are standard. Switch to first names with managers or senior colleagues once they signal that preference or they give you permission to use it (this "permission" may be as subtle as simply signing an email with their first name).

Bad Example:

hi just wondering if we can meet Friday? I'm free at 1, 3, and 4:30. Let me know if any of those work for you. thanks.

Better Example:

Subject: Follow-Up and Meeting Availability

Hi Carter,

It was a pleasure speaking with you this morning. I'm looking forward to connecting in person.

I'm available to meet on Friday at the following times:

−1:00-2:00 p.m.

−3:00-4:00 p.m.

−4:30-5:30 p.m.

Please let me know what time works best for you, and whether you'd prefer to meet at your office or at a nearby coffee shop.

Best regards,

Jordan

Internal Communication Tools (Slack, Teams, etc.)

Professionalism & Tone

- Messages feel casual, but they're part of the company record. Don't say anything you wouldn't say in an email.

- Keep language concise, respectful, and professional. Avoid slang, sarcasm, or inside jokes that could be misunderstood.

- Pay attention to how your manager and team write (formal vs. casual, detailed vs. brief) and adapt to match.

Be Respectful

- Use @mentions selectively and only tag people who truly need to see it. Overusing @channel or @here can frustrate coworkers.

  I was on a team where there was one individual who constantly used @mentions to ask questions to large groups of people in public channels. Doing this made others perceive this individual as being lazy (asking questions without trying to figure out the answer first) and disrespectful (constantly bothering many people with notifications). Although this seems small, it quickly became a large part of that individual's reputation. Don't be that person.

- Post in channels for visibility, but use DMs for sensitive messages or messages that are only relevant to the recipient.
- Put your full question or update in one well-written message instead of multiple one-liners. Sending multiple messages in a row can be annoying to others, and they may make others think that you are scatterbrained or unorganized.

Timing & Responsiveness

- Don't expect instant replies. People are busy, in meetings, or in different time zones.
- Respect off-hours. Use message scheduling if you're drafting outside of normal working hours.
- Effectively use status updates. Instead of "In a meeting," write "On a client call, back at 3 p.m." Respect others' Do Not Disturb.
- Update progress without being asked. Quick updates, such as *"Draft 1 is done. The next step is Finance review—will update tomorrow,"* help provide transparency and are appreciated by coworkers and managers.

Clarity & Efficiency

- Be direct by putting the most important request or update first.
- Avoid burying multiple requests in one ping. One ask per message is a good rule of thumb.
- If a discussion becomes lengthy, post a short recap or next steps.

Culture & Social Norms

- Use emojis (✅ 👀 👍) for a purpose like acknowledgment, but avoid overloading professional threads with them.

- Some teams are GIF-heavy, others buttoned-up. Match the culture.

- Always acknowledge when someone responds to you, even with a simple reaction. Not acknowledging can be perceived as ghosting or being unresponsive.

- Thank people in the thread or channel (not just DM), so contributions are visible.

Information Sharing

- Use links instead of attachments when possible, so others always get the latest version.

- Add context by explaining what a link or file is and why it matters.

- Double-check before posting in large or company-wide channels to avoid making embarrassing errors.

- If you find a helpful document, template, or article, drop it in with a line of context; it shows initiative and adds value.

Building Credibility & Visibility

- Your Slack/Teams presence is a reflection of your professionalism. Clear writing, respectful tagging, and being responsive build trust.

- If you've put in some effort to find an answer but still can't figure it out, tag someone who can, because it shows resourcefulness.

- Answering questions in open channels builds visibility and credibility. It's a great way to be helpful in a public setting.

Wrap-Up: The Unspoken Expectations of Professional Communication

Being prepared means more than following the rules. It means knowing what's expected even when no one spells it out.

Emails

- **Rule:** Send a message to get your point across.
- **Expectation:** Write clear, structured messages that show respect for your reader's time. Proofread, use proper greetings, and write as if your message could be forwarded because it might be.

Texting

- **Rule:** Keep it short and appropriate.
- **Expectation:** Be concise and professional. Skip the slang, consider the timing, and always lead with clarity.

Phone & Voicemail

- **Rule:** Answer and return calls.
- **Expectation:** Speak clearly, return calls promptly, and leave voicemails that are concise, confident, and complete.

Verbal Communication

- **Rule:** Speak with purpose.
- **Expectation:** Speak with confidence, listen actively, avoid filler language, and match your communication style to the setting and audience.

Small Talk & Introductions

- **Rule:** Be polite when meeting someone new.
- **Expectation:** Smile, make eye contact, and introduce yourself with intention. Use small talk to build connections. Show genuine interest and remember names.

Internal Communication (Slack, Teams, etc.)

- **Rule:** Be responsive.
- **Expectation:** Be thoughtful with your tone, tagging, and timing. Keep your messages clear, useful, and aligned with team culture.

Final Takeaway

Every message you send, every word you speak, and every interaction you have shapes how others perceive your professionalism. Employers are listening to what you say, and they're paying close attention to how you say it.

Communication is one of the most sought-after skills in any workplace, so consistently improving how you show up (both in person and online) will make you a more confident communicator and a stronger professional.

The Unspoken Expectations of Networking: Turning Conversations Into Relationships and Opportunities

The goal of networking is to build real connections and relationships. It's not what you know, but who you know, that can really get you ahead by opening up opportunities you might otherwise not have had. Networking can be done in structured, preplanned settings (such as career fairs), casual, unplanned settings (like at a football game), or online (like on LinkedIn).

Why Networking Matters

Many students think applying online is the key to getting hired, but up to 70% of jobs are never even posted.[7] The majority of roles are filled through internal promotions, employee referrals, and networking connections.

By building relationships, you gain access to opportunities most students never see.

The more connections you have, the more chances you have to land internships and jobs, especially those not publicly posted. In

---

[7] Joseph Willmott, "The Hidden Job Market: Why 70% of Job Opportunities Are Never Posted-and What You Can Do about It," WBN News, March 10, 2025, https://www.wbn.digital/the-hidden-job-market-why-70-of-job-opportunities-are-never-posted-and-what-you-can-do-about-it/.

fact, nearly 80% of professionals say that networking is essential to their career success.[8]

What Are Referrals and Why Do They Matter?

A referral is when someone at a company recommends you for a role, either by submitting your name through an internal system or introducing you directly to a hiring manager or recruiter. If a referral is hired, the referrer typically gets a monetary bonus.

Here's why they're powerful:

- Referrals 4x your chances of getting an offer.[9] Recruiters trust referrals more than cold applications because you're seen as pre-vetted.

- Referral candidates often bypass résumé scanners and get directly reviewed by humans.

- Referrals are hired 7x faster than applicants from job boards.[10]

- Referrals are based more on relationships and less on qualifications. They typically occur through networking, such as coffee chats, LinkedIn connections, and alumni introductions. Even a brief professional interaction (e.g., coffee

---

[8] LinkedIn Corporate Communications, "Eighty-Percent of Professionals Consider Networking Important to Career Success," LinkedIn Pressroom, accessed October 1, 2025, https://news.linkedin.com/2017/6/eighty-percent-of-professionals-consider-networking-important-to-career-success.

[9] Jack Flynn, "25 Incredible Employee Referral Statistics [2023]: Facts about Employee Referrals in the U.S.," Zippia, June 28, 2023, https://www.zippia.com/advice/employee-referral-statistics/.

[10] Marissa Wilson, "Referrals Are 7x More Likely to Be Hired than Job Board Candidates," Pinpoint, September 4, 2024, https://www.pinpointhq.com/insights/referrals-are-7x-more-likely-to-be-hired-than-job-board-candidates/.

chat) can lead to a referral if the person is impressed by how you present yourself.

Below is an example of how a connection helped me get my foot in the door at a competitive company. Especially in bigger companies that get flooded with résumés from exceptional candidates, utilizing relationships is one way to ensure your résumé gets looked at. It goes back to the importance of realizing that it's not always what you know, but who you know.

In this example, I applied for a position and highlighted a project I worked on in collaboration with the company's current employees. I then reached out to one of my connections just to reconnect and let him know that I applied for a position (without any specific ask from him). This led him to offer a referral for me. I could've just submitted the application, but making the extra effort to leverage a relationship proved to be invaluable.

Andrew ✅ (He/Him) · 6:48 PM

Alright, I'll find out who's the recruiter and hiring manager and put in a good word for you. It would be awesome to have you working for ██████.

Lindsay Muench 🔗 · 7:13 PM

Wow, that would be great and much appreciated. Thanks so much, Andy!

In-Person Networking Events: Tips to Maximize Your Time

- Attend events to meet new people. This could be anything from a career fair put on by your business school to a philanthropy event hosted by a local group that you support. Find events that interest you because it's easier to connect with people when you share common ground.

- If a company you're interested in is on campus, go to every event they attend. Showing up consistently (even at back-to-back events, such as a reception the evening before a career fair) shows genuine interest and makes you more memorable.

- During internships, attend all events and meet as many new people as you can. This is one of the best ways to get as much out of the experience as possible, even if you don't receive a return offer.

- Preview the attendee list if possible. Utilize LinkedIn to become familiar with faces, names, titles, and backgrounds. Research two to three people or companies of interest in advance and have one or two thoughtful questions ready to show genuine interest.

- Name tags should be printed with a legible font and worn on your chest on your right-hand side. The reason it's placed there is that when you meet someone, you extend your right hand. This naturally turns your upper body slightly to the right, which positions your name tag directly in the other person's line of sight.

If you are responsible for writing your own name tag, make sure your penmanship is legible and large enough for others to read.

I've seen people put nametags in unusual places. I once saw a woman with her nametag on her thigh. Her shirt was silk, and she didn't want to risk ruining it, so she thought her leg was the best alternative. Bottom line: if you're attending an event where you'll be wearing a nametag, don't wear fabrics or outfits you'd hesitate to put one on.

- First impressions are based on appearance and body language, so dress appropriately for the networking event. If it's a casual event, such as at a tailgate, don't feel like you need to be dressed in business attire.

- A smile is the quickest way to break the ice and convey an approachable demeanor.

- Find a commonality quickly. It could be your school, your major, an organization, the venue, the city, hobbies, common acquaintances, etc. Shared interests make conversations easier and more memorable.

- Never underestimate the importance of a good, firm handshake and eye contact.

- Never be afraid or hesitant to introduce yourself.

- Move throughout the room to meet, greet, and converse. Don't fall into the comfort zone of talking to only people you know or standing in the same spot.

- If you attend an event alone and find yourself uncomfortable, here are a few of my tricks:
  - Go to the food buffet or the line for beverages, as these are easy places to make small talk.

- If the event has booths, walk up to a booth that interests you. This is a great way to transition from mingling alone to getting the first conversation under your belt.

- Groups of three or more are easier to approach than a group of two.

- Prepare yourself for small talk by reviewing current events, industry news, etc.

- Remove stirrers from your beverage before taking a sip. The stirrer is not a mini straw.

- While standing, hold your beverage in your left hand, so your right one is free to receive or initiate a handshake, and it is not cold or wet.

- Select user-friendly appetizers that can be eaten neatly in one or two bites.

- Remember that at professional events, your social skills and actions reflect the school or company you represent.

- Don't behave differently to different audiences. Treat everyone you meet, from hiring managers to business leaders and servers, with kindness and respect.

- End a conversation with a sincere, gracious statement such as: "It's been a pleasure speaking with you, please excuse me," or "I have enjoyed our conversation, please excuse me."

- If you are a guest, thank your host before leaving the event.

LinkedIn and Online Networking: Make a Strong Online First Impression

Your online presence matters because 70% of employers check a candidate's social media presence before making a hiring decision.[11] That means your online presence might be their first impression of you.

First Step: Clean Up Your Social Profiles

Here's what to look for (and fix) on public social media accounts:

1. **Photos & Videos**

   Remove or archive anything you wouldn't want an employer or professor to see. That includes party pictures, revealing outfits, or anything involving illegal or irresponsible behavior.

2. **Captions & Comments**

   Delete posts or comments with foul language, offensive jokes, inappropriate hashtags, or complaints about school or work.

3. **Usernames, Handles & Bios**

   Avoid immature or inappropriate names (e.g., @partygurl47). Keep bios free of controversial topics, sarcasm, and profanity.

4. **Privacy Settings**

   If you want to keep a personal account private, make sure you have the correct settings selected. Even if you

---

[11] "Social Media Integral to Recruiting as Most Businesses Use It to Source, Research and Screen Candidates," ExpressPros.com., accessed October 1, 2025, https://www.prweb.com/releases/social-media-integral-to-recruiting-as-most-businesses-use-it-to-source-research-and-screen-candidates-828377504.html.

have the correct privacy settings, still assume nothing is 100% private; recruiters sometimes view mutual content through others.

Pro Tips: Google yourself to make sure nothing unexpected comes up. Also check your public Spotify playlists for inappropriate titles, and your Venmo history for inappropriate language or topics (set it to private).

LinkedIn Basics

Not having a LinkedIn profile can be seen as a red flag. Employers expect to find you, so it's important to set up a strong profile before you start networking and applying for internships. Make sure your profile is complete with a professional picture, a clear headline, and an about section, as well as details about your experiences. Keep in mind that even if your experiences aren't directly relevant to the internships you're interested in, just having experiences in general shows responsibility, initiative, and skills that employers value.

Once you've created a complete profile, start by connecting with people you already know, then branch out strategically.

Who to Connect With First

Friends

Even though LinkedIn is a professional network, connecting with friends is valuable. It helps you follow their career journeys and expands and strengthens your overall network.

Classmates

Whether you worked together on a group project or just shared a class, it's smart to connect. As alumni, your paths may cross again, and your shared college experience creates a natural networking opportunity later on.

Professors and Academic Advisors

These mentors can write strong LinkedIn recommendations and often have wide networks in the industries they teach. As you progress in your career, you can also add value to their network as an alum in their field.

Coaches, Bosses, and Club Leaders

These individuals can also serve as great LinkedIn references. Staying connected gives you reasons to keep in touch over time, whether it's congratulating them on a promotion, a big win, or sharing your own updates.

Internship Coworkers

Intern peers are valuable contacts because they're often pursuing similar career paths. As you move into new roles, you can help each other network and navigate job opportunities in your shared industry.

Family, Friends, and Neighbors

These connections often know you personally and have more established networks. If they're aware of your interests, they can serve as trusted advocates and connectors in your career journey.

Alumni from Your High School and College

Alumni networks are one of the most powerful resources available to you. Be proactive about connecting and be ready to offer help to others when you can.

Tips for Maximizing Online Networking

Step 1: Engage with Their Profile Before You Connect

Before sending a connection request, increase the chances they recognize you and accept the connection request.

- View their profile.
- Like one or two of their recent posts, or leave a thoughtful comment.

This puts you on their radar. When they see your name or face in their connection requests, you'll feel less like a stranger.

Step 2: Don't Connect Without a Reason

Strangers (even from your school or company) still need context. If there's no clear reason to connect, don't. Networking isn't about collecting contacts; it's about building relevant connections.

Pro tip: If you haven't met, you *must* explain why you're reaching out.

Example of a good message (personalized, relevant, and brief):

> *Hi Tim, I'm a freshman at Michigan exploring finance internships. I saw that you were also a finance major at Michigan and have been in a variety of finance roles since your internship at UBS. I'd love to connect.*

Example of a bad message:

> Just hitting "Connect" with no explanation.

Step 3: Personalize Every Request

Copy-paste messages get ignored. Always tailor your message:

- Introduce yourself and why you're reaching out.
- Mention what you have in common or what caught your attention.
- Keep it concise (LinkedIn has character limits).
- Be clear and friendly.

Below is a great example of a cold LinkedIn outreach I received. I did not have anyone in common with this individual, but she provided a clear reason for why she was looking to connect. I could tell that her message was personalized to me, and there was a clear ask for what she was looking for, so it warranted a response. After our conversation, she got an interview with HubSpot, which led to a job offer she accepted!

Kristen 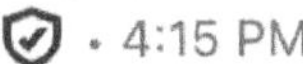 · 4:15 PM

Hi Lindsay! I saw a few CSM openings at Hubspot that I thought looked really interesting and wanted to reach out to hear about your experience and journey. I used to be a CSM at Workday and am currently an AE at Salesforce. I LOVE helping customers and my customers rave about their awesome support!

Be a Connector, Even Early In Your Career

Networking isn't just about *getting* help; it's also about *adding* value. One of the best ways to build trust and long-term visibility is by connecting others.

Introduce two people who could benefit from knowing each other. Even if you're just getting started, don't underestimate your value. Maybe you know a classmate looking for finance internships, and you have a friend who just interned at J.P. Morgan. A quick introduction could help them both, and they'll remember who made it happen.

A real-world example of this was when a friend from college reached out to me because his fiancée was interested in making a career pivot, and he thought she could benefit from speaking with me. You can also see he used a personalized, sincere opening, which made me even more receptive to his request. Being a connector is a great way to provide value and stay in touch with others.

Evan　　　✅ · 9:07 AM

Lindsay, I see you have a new last name! Congratulations to you and Dylan! My fiancee Sam is looking to transition to a career in Customer Success, and has had a few interviews. Do you think I could send this to her and perhaps you two can chat? It would mean the world!

Start the "5-Minute Favor" Habit

If you dedicate just five minutes a week to nurturing your network, especially when you're just beginning your career, you'll stand out without overwhelming yourself.

This idea was popularized by Adam Rifkin, a successful entrepreneur once named *Fortune's* Best Networker. He's known for practicing what he calls "5-minute favors," which are quick, meaningful actions. Organizational psychologist Adam Grant shared this concept in his bestselling book *Give and Take,* noting how Rifkin used small favors to build a powerful, trusted network over time.[12]

Here are examples of ways to practice the 5-Minute Favor:

- *Endorse a skill on LinkedIn:* Visit a connection's profile and click "endorse" next to a skill they've listed (like public speaking, Excel, marketing, etc.). It's a quick way to show support that people will notice.

- *Share someone's post*: Reshare a post from someone in your network, adding a quick comment about why you found it valuable.

- *Leave a thoughtful comment*: Go beyond "Congrats!" Add a short insight, question, or compliment that shows you actually read the post.

- *Send a helpful resource*: If you read an article, hear a podcast, or see a program that someone in your network would benefit from, send it their way with a short message.

- *Mention opportunities*: If you see an internship opening, a student program, or a campus event that could help someone you know, pass it along. It shows you're thinking of them, and it builds goodwill.

---

[12] Adam Grant, *Give and Take: Why Helping Others Drives Our Success* (New York, United States: Penguin Books, 2013).

Coffee Chats: How to Learn, Connect, and Get Referred

What It Is

A coffee chat is a casual 20- to 30-minute conversation designed to learn. It's one of the most effective, low-pressure ways you can use to build your network and learn from those a few steps ahead of you. These are sometimes referred to as informational interviews.

You can use coffee chats to learn about:

- A college major or program
- A specific company or industry
- Career paths and real-world experiences (these conversations help you figure out what you want to do by hearing how and why others chose certain careers, companies, etc.)

If done well, coffee chats often lead to helpful insights, mentorships, future introductions, and sometimes referrals.

Step 1: Find People

- Peers, alumni, or young professionals
- People with shared interests or backgrounds
- Individuals in roles or industries that interest you
- Family friends, neighbors, or relatives

Pro Tip: Focus on people one to two steps ahead of you. This doesn't necessarily mean "one grade above." It means those who recently did what you're about to do (e.g., recent grads in entry-level roles).

Where to Look:

- Ask people you know for introductions
- Use LinkedIn filters to find people by school, job title, company, or location

Pro Tip: Use LinkedIn's Alumni Tool (found on your school's LinkedIn page) to filter graduates by company, job title, or location. It's one of the fastest ways to find people who already share something in common with you.

Step 2: Reach Out

Keep your message short, clear, and respectful. Don't overthink it.

Example LinkedIn connection request:

> *Hi Matt. I'm a sophomore at Elon exploring sales and marketing careers. I noticed you're a recent alum, and I'd love to connect and learn about your experience at HubSpot!*

Once they accept, send a follow-up message to ask for a chat:

> *Thanks for connecting, Matt! I'm really interested in sales roles at marketing tech companies, and your path from an agency internship to HubSpot stood out to me. Would you be open to a quick 15- to 20-minute chat sometime next week? I'd really appreciate your insights.*

Step 3: Prepare

- Send a calendar invite (assume it's a phone call unless told otherwise).

- Make the subject line clear (Dylan <> Matt - Marketing Careers).
- Make the location clear (Dylan to call Matt at [phone number]).
- Research the person's background.
- Draft five to seven thoughtful questions.
- Practice your elevator pitch.

Step 4: Lead the Conversation

- Be on time and start with gratitude.
- Begin with light small talk and your 30-second intro. For example:

"Hi [Name], thanks again for taking the time to speak with me today. I really appreciate it."

(Pause for them to respond and then ask an opener like "How's your week going?" or "Are things pretty busy at work right now?" to ease into the conversation.)

Then transition into your introduction/elevator pitch:

"I'm a sophomore at Elon, majoring in marketing, and I'm currently part of our student sales team, where we compete in roleplays and work with real company sponsors. I've really enjoyed the hands-on experience, especially learning how to build relationships with clients and ask better questions. I've started exploring internships in tech sales, and your path stood out to me because you made the move from retail sales into a tech company, which is something I've been really curious about. I'd love to hear more about what that transition looked like and any advice you have for students like me trying to break into tech sales."

- Ask the questions you prepared, but be comfortable asking questions off-script if relevant.
- Take notes.
- Wrap up a few minutes early.
- Ask: "Is there anyone else you'd recommend I speak to?" Do not ask for a job!

Step 5: Follow Up

- Send a thank-you email within 24 hours.
- Reference something specific you learned or appreciated.
- Close the loop and share how you'll act on their advice.

Example message:

Thanks again for your time today. I'm going to look into [resource they mentioned] and start working on [skill they suggested]. I'll follow up in a month to let you know how it goes. I really appreciated your perspective!

Pro Tip: Send a 30-day update. Almost no one does this, and it's how you turn a one-time conversation into long-term relationships.

Note: Coffee chats can be leveraged during internships. Use coffee breaks and lunch hours to "get beyond small talk" with other employees. As long as it's not interrupting your actual job that needs to get done, reaching out to others and getting 15 to 20 minutes on the calendar with them is a great use of your time.

Sparking Offline Connections: Make Everyday Interactions Count

You never know where a meaningful conversation might start, and sometimes, the smallest details can open the door.

Wear, carry, or use visible conversation starters in public, like:

- Hats, sweatshirts, laptop stickers, mugs, etc., with a college, hometown, or sports team logo
- Items that show your personal interests (e.g., water bottle with your running club name on it, key chain from your favorite travel destination, etc.)

Why it works:

These subtle cues often spark spontaneous conversations with people who share something in common, whether it's an alum from your school, a fan of the same team, or someone who shares a common interest.

Example:

Wearing a UVA hat at the airport could lead to a quick chat with a UVA alum who now works at a company you're interested in.

Pro Tip:

Be ready with a simple elevator pitch or question when someone engages you. A friendly "Did you go to [school] too?" or "Are you in [industry] as well?" can naturally lead into a networking moment even if it doesn't start out as one.

How to Maintain Your Network: How to Stay Connected (Without Being Annoying)

Networking doesn't stop after the first message or coffee chat. The real value comes from how you nurture relationships over time; however, only 48% of professionals actively maintain their network even though the large majority agree on the value of doing so.[13]

1. Stay Organized

Relationships are built on personal connection, and remembering the little details is key.

Use a simple tracker or spreadsheet to record:

- Name, school/company, and job title (if applicable)
- How you connected (LinkedIn, referral, webinar, coffee chat, etc.)
- Date of last interaction
- Personal notes like shared interests, hometowns, sports teams, family details, advice they gave, or anything memorable from your chat
- Next step or follow-up reminder (e.g., "Reach out in spring," "Send article about AI in marketing," etc.)

Why this matters: When you reach out again, even if it's months later, you'll sound thoughtful and intentional, not random or transactional.

---

[13] LinkedIn Corporate Communications, "Eighty-Percent of Professionals Consider Networking Important to Career Success," LinkedIn Pressroom, accessed October 1, 2025, https://news.linkedin.com/2017/6/eighty-percent-of-professionals-consider-networking-important-to-career-success.

2. Reconnect Thoughtfully

When it's time to follow up, don't dive in asking for a favor.

What NOT to say:

> Hi Jim. I know it's been a while since we talked, but I'm interested in an internship at Google. I know you've been there for a few years, so I was hoping you could help me out. Can we schedule a call?

- Sounds transactional and abrupt
- Leads with the ask instead of rebuilding the relationship
- Doesn't acknowledge the time gap

What to say instead:

> Hi Jim, I hope you're doing well! I can't believe it's been almost a year since we last connected. I remember you were celebrating a Packers win back then. Are you planning on going to any games this season?
>
> I saw that Google just posted a new marketing internship for sophomores, and it reminded me of the advice you shared about building early experience in tech. Would you be open to a quick chat or possibly pointing me toward someone on the team who knows more about the program?
>
> Thanks in advance. I really appreciate it!

- Rebuilds rapport with a personal reference
- Acknowledges the time gap gracefully
- Frames the request respectfully without pressure

- Offers options, not obligations
- Ends with appreciation

Here's a real-life example from a college friend who reached out to me after we hadn't been in touch for a while. Her message was kind, personable, and clear about what she was asking for. That's the kind of outreach people are most likely to respond to. It's also a perfect reminder of why staying connected on LinkedIn matters. Since we hadn't spoken in years, the only way she knew I worked at this company was because we were connected there.

Jo Beth (She/Her) · 4:43 PM

Hi Lindsay!!! Hope all is well!! I saw that you recently got married this year–congratulations!! You were a stunning bride!

I saw an opening ███████████████████ at the ████ ██████ and was curious if you enjoy working there. Thank you for your insight!!! 🤍

3. Make Thoughtful Touchpoints

Good networking is proactive, not just reactive. Stay in touch by looking for small ways to stay top-of-mind without asking for anything.

Great reasons to reach out:

- Share a milestone or update ("Just landed my first internship. Thanks for your help and advice!").
- Send a podcast, article, or opportunity they might like.

- Congratulate them on a promotion or new role.
- Follow up on a past conversation or reference.
- Message them when something reminds you of them ("Saw this and thought of your tip about …").

These moments build trust, and they remind people you're not only interested in what they can do for you.

Pro Tip: The notes section of the contact record in your phone can also be helpful in managing professional relationships (see example below). Adding information unique to the individual will make you stand out when you reach out to them. It will feel authentic and personable.

4. Stay Involved

Some of the best connections happen naturally, outside of formal networking events. Staying active in different circles keeps relationships warm and opens the door to unexpected opportunities.

Ways to stay connected:

- Alumni events, Facebook groups, LinkedIn groups, or Slack channels
- Holiday card exchanges
- Reunions for student organizations, volunteer groups, or former teams
- Interest-based groups like: book clubs, pickleball leagues, art classes, running clubs, etc.

Even casual interactions like these can re-spark relationships, lead to introductions, or keep you top of mind with people in your field.

Pro Tip: Talk about your internship search in everyday conversations. Be specific: role, industry, location, timing, etc. The clearer you are, the easier it is for people to connect you to opportunities they might know about.

Wrap-Up: The Unspoken Expectations of Networking

Being prepared means more than following the rules. It means knowing what's expected even when no one spells it out.

Referrals

- **Rule:** Ask someone to recommend you.
- **Expectation:** Earn referrals through genuine relationships, consistent professionalism, and leaving others impressed enough to vouch for you. Be appreciative and willing to help others.

In-Person Networking

- **Rule:** Show up to events and meet people.
- **Expectation:** Arrive prepared with research, move beyond your comfort zone, and engage with confidence (e.g., firm handshake, thoughtful questions, and good body language).

LinkedIn & Online Presence

- **Rule:** Have a profile.
- **Expectation:** Build a personal brand online that highlights your strengths. Build meaningful connections and make an effort to add value to those in your network.

Coffee Chats

- **Rule:** Schedule meetings with people who interest you.

- **Expectation:** Come prepared with questions, listen actively, respect time, and follow up with gratitude and updates that show you acted on their advice.

Maintaining Your Network

- **Rule:** Reach out to others.

- **Expectation:** Stay organized, follow up thoughtfully, and create value for others so your network becomes a lasting source of trust and opportunity.

Final Takeaway

Networking is about cultivating trust and building relationships, not just collecting contacts. You don't need hundreds of connections; you just need genuine ones. And the earlier you start building those relationships, before you *need* them, the more powerful they'll become when you do.

Remember:

- **Be consistent.** One conversation isn't enough. It's important to keep showing up.

- **Be helpful.** Share resources, make introductions, ask meaningful questions.

- **Be thoughtful.** Take notes, follow up, and remember the details that matter.

- **Be appreciative.** Gratitude makes people want to keep helping.

The Unspoken Expectations of Interviews: What Employers Notice But Don't Tell You

Landing the interview means your résumé stood out, so now it's about proving yourself in person. Remember, interviewers are people too. While they're assessing your qualifications, they're equally assessing how you show up, how you connect with others, how you carry yourself, and how you follow up.

These factors are often the deciding factor between a rejection and an offer because opportunities often go to the most prepared, not always the smartest or most experienced.

It's important to remember that you are also assessing if this opportunity is a fit for you. If the company and interviewers don't treat you the way you deserve to be treated, or if the opportunity ends up being something you're not very interested in, you can politely decline moving forward in the process.

Preparation Checklist: What Really Helps You Get Hired

1. Basic Interview Prep

Interviewers can quickly tell who skimmed the company website the night before and who's actually prepared to contribute.

- Research the company's mission, culture, recent news, and core products and services. Use their website, LinkedIn, and recent press releases.

- Look up your interviewer(s) on LinkedIn. Know their role and background so you can personalize your questions.

- Know your résumé line by line, especially any numbers, projects, or leadership roles.

- Know the job description well enough to be able to communicate how you can add value.

- Prepare three to five strong questions to ask at the end. Focus on specifics like team dynamics, challenges, or how success is measured, instead of questions you could Google the answer to or generic questions you could ask in any interview.

- Know your "why." Be able to clearly articulate:
  - Why this company?
  - Why this role?
  - Why now?
  - Why you?

2. *Professional Presence and Appearance*

Your appearance is the first impression you give before you even speak. It should show that you respect the opportunity and understand the professional setting.

- Wear clean, well-fitting clothes that match the company culture. If you're unsure about the dress code, ask the recruiter directly.

- Iron or steam your outfit the night before because wrinkles suggest carelessness. Use a lint roller if necessary.

- Keep hair neat, nails trimmed, and shoes polished or clean.

- Avoid applying heavy perfume/cologne and wearing distracting patterns or accessories.

- Don't chew gum, carry a water bottle, or wear sunglasses on your head.

- Lay out everything the night before, including socks, belt, and backup options, so nothing distracts you before the interview. To be certain you'll be prepared, it's smart to make sure you have all the clothing and accessories you need soon after you schedule the interview, in case you need to purchase something or get anything dry-cleaned.

- Refer to the Dress Code section in "The Unspoken Expectations of Professionalism" chapter for additional tips.

3. First Impressions and Body Language

People decide whether they trust and respect you within seconds, and most of that is based on nonverbal cues.

- Stand and sit tall to improve presence and project confidence.
- Make eye contact when listening *and* speaking (but don't stare).
- Nod occasionally to show engagement, and match your expression to your tone.
- Start and end the interview with a firm handshake: Two to three pumps, full web-to-web contact, direct eye contact, and a confident "Nice to meet you."
- Avoid fidgeting, pen-clicking, leg bouncing, or shifting in your seat.
- Refer to both the First Impressions and Body Language sections in "The Unspoken Expectations of Professionalism" chapter for additional tips.

4. Communication

Interviews are not just about the answers you give. They're about how you carry on a conversation and whether you come across as someone who can represent the company well.

- Practice your answer to "Tell me about yourself" out loud. Use the structure for your two-minute elevator pitch outlined in "The Unspoken Expectations of Professional Communication" chapter. Make sure your pitch is relevant to the specific opportunity you're interviewing for. Nailing this introduction will set a strong tone for the rest of the interview.

- Show enthusiasm about the opportunity. People want to hire people who are excited about the role and the company.
- To convey more confidence, speak clearly and at a measured pace, as nervousness often causes people to rush, ramble, or mumble.
- Avoid filler words: "like," "um," and "you know."
- Use the other person's name occasionally to create connection and reinforce engagement.
- Thank each interviewer for their time and consideration at the end of each interview.
- Refer to "The Unspoken Expectations of Professional Communication" chapter for additional tips.

5. Punctuality

Being late, even just once during the interview process, can signal unreliability or a lack of seriousness. On time is late. Early is prepared.

- Plan your route and backup plan the day before (it's important to know parking, traffic, or building access rules).
- Arrive early and check in 5 to 10 minutes before the interview start time.
- If you're running late, communicate immediately with a polite, brief message:

  "Hi [Name], I'm so sorry. I'm running behind due to [brief reason], but I'm on my way and should arrive by [time]. I appreciate your patience."

- If it's virtual interviews:
  - Test your tech 30 minutes before (Wi-Fi, camera, mic, lighting).
  - Log in three to five minutes early. Waiting in the "lobby" is expected and appreciated.

Day-Of Logistics: Don't Let Small Mistakes Cost You

Do Not Bring a Parent

- Bringing a parent, even to walk in with you, immediately shows a lack of independence and readiness for the workplace.
- Employers will assume you can't handle professional environments on your own, and many will disqualify you.

Confirm Location and Logistics

- Look up the exact address, building name, suite number, and parking instructions the night before.
  - If you're unfamiliar with the area, consider doing a practice run if it's local (or use Google Maps to estimate real-time travel with traffic).
- Make sure you know the interviewer's name so you can properly ask for them at the front desk when you arrive.
- If it's virtual:
  - Test Zoom/Google Meet link
  - Check Wi-Fi, webcam, microphone, and background

Arrive 5 to 10 Minutes Early (Not Sooner)

- Arriving early shows respect, but more than 10 minutes early can feel disruptive.

- If you're too early, wait in your car or outside until 5 to 10 minutes before your scheduled time.

- Focus on the time you need to leave for the interview, not the actual interview time. Allow yourself an extra 5 to 10 minutes for possible delays. If you are going to be late, give notice to the person you're interviewing with.

Silence All Tech Before Entering

- Disable smartwatch notifications and put your phone on airplane mode, or simply shut it off.

- Do this before you walk in the door, not while sitting in the reception area.

- Put your phone in your bag (instead of your pocket) to avoid the habit of checking it.

Know How to Handle Beverages Professionally

- If they offer you a beverage:
  - It's perfectly okay to politely accept *or* decline water, coffee, soda, or tea if offered.
  - Don't stir, slurp, or fidget with the cup while speaking.
  - At the end of the interview, politely ask: "Would you like me to leave this here or take it back to the kitchen?" This shows consideration and leaves a final positive impression.

- If you bring your own water bottle:
  - Keep it in your bag or briefcase (*not* on the desk or table).
  - Only take it out in case of emergency (e.g., coughing fit), and then place it back discreetly.

Remember: The Interview Starts the Moment You Arrive

- Be friendly, polite, and professional to everyone, including:
  - Receptionist or front desk staff
  - Security guards
  - Other people in the lobby or on the elevator
- Be mindful of what you're saying. For example, if you are on the phone in the lobby or elevator, be aware that the person next to you could be the hiring manager.

During college, I was in line getting coffee with a friend who casually admitted she wasn't ready for her interview later that day and wasn't too worried because she didn't really want the internship. Neither of us thought much of it until she texted me later to say the woman standing behind us in line turned out to be her interviewer. Needless to say, no matter what she said or did in the interview, she wasn't getting the offer. It's a powerful reminder to always be mindful of your environment and what you say or do, especially when you're interviewing.

Adapting to Different Interview Formats: Have Confidence No Matter the Setting

Interview formats may vary, but the expectations stay the same. Whether you're meeting on Zoom or recording answers for an AI platform, you'll be judged on professionalism, communication, and presence.

Virtual Interviews (Zoom, Teams, Google Meet)

Hiring managers expect you to show up with the same level of professionalism, preparation, and presence you'd bring to an in-person interview.

Camera On

- Always turn your camera on, unless the recruiter *explicitly* tells you otherwise.
- Camera-off shows disengagement or a lack of preparation in an interview setting.

Dress the Part

- Dress professionally, even below the waist, because you may need to stand unexpectedly.
- Avoid any distracting patterns or colors.

Background + Lighting Matter

- Choose a neutral, uncluttered background.
- Face a window or light source for natural lighting (don't sit with your back to it).
- Avoid distracting backgrounds or virtual filters.

Simulate Eye Contact

- Look into the webcam, not at your own video feed.
- Position your camera at eye level to avoid unflattering angles and improve engagement.

Test Your Tech Early

- Check:
  - Microphone
  - Camera
  - Wi-Fi signal strength
  - Login links and time zones
- Many video conference platforms have installations required before use (or to optimize use). Make sure you have everything installed properly before starting the interview.

Eliminate Distractions

- Silence:
  - Phone
  - Smartwatch
  - Computer notifications (Texts, Slack, Teams, pop-ups)
- Close all tabs or apps not related to the interview
- Ask roommates or family to be quiet during your interview window

AI Interviews (HireVue, Spark Hire, etc.)

AI interviews are often one-way video recordings. You'll answer timed prompts on camera, and your responses are reviewed later by humans *and/or* AI software.

Perform Like It's Live

- Speak with energy, warmth, and clarity as if someone's watching you in real time.
- Smile, maintain eye contact with the camera, and project enthusiasm.
- Avoid reading notes or sounding scripted. AI can often detect monotone delivery.

Timing & Pausing

- Most platforms give you 30 to 60 seconds to think before the timer starts.
- Don't panic: pause, collect your thoughts, then speak confidently.
- Aim for one- to two-minute answers: clear, concise, and focused. Avoid rushing and rambling.

Pro Tips:

- Practice with demo AI interview tools or record yourself answering prompts.
- Use keywords from the job description (AI often scans for alignment).
- Speak in full sentences with a clear beginning, middle, and end.
- Keep your tone friendly and confident.

Following Up with Thank-You Notes: What to Say and When to Say It

Sending a thank-you note after an interview is one of the simplest ways to stand out professionally and show maturity, gratitude, and continued interest in the role.

Why It Matters

- 86% of hiring managers say thank-you notes influence their decision-making.[14]
- 57% of job seekers don't send a thank-you note.[15]

That means writing one instantly puts you ahead of most candidates.

When to Send Thank-You Notes

Send your thank-you notes within 24 hours of your Interview—ideally, later that day (after business hours) or the following morning. The sooner you follow up, the more memorable and thoughtful it feels. If you are handwriting a thank-you note, you can still send a thank-you email within the first 24 hours. However, do not send an email immediately after an interview because that's perceived as merely "checking the box," which feels less sincere.

---

[14] "Thank-You Notes Can Tip Scale in Job Candidates' Favor, yet Few Write Them," Thank-You Notes Can Tip Scale in Job Candidates' Favor, Yet Few Write Them - Nov 20, 2017, accessed October 1, 2025, https://press.roberthalf.com/2017-11-20-Thank-You-Notes-Can-Tip-Scale-in-Job-Candidates-Favor-Yet-Few-Write-Them.

[15] These 5 simple mistakes could be costing you the job, accessed October 1, 2025, https://www.careerbuilder.com/advice/blog/these-5-simple-mistakes-could-be-costing-you-the-job.

Who to Thank and How

Write a separate thank-you to each person you interviewed with. If it were a panel interview, still thank everyone on the panel. If you don't know their email addresses, ask the recruiter politely and double-check on LinkedIn for name spelling.

For in-person interviews, a handwritten thank-you note is ideal. For virtual interviews, email is perfectly acceptable.

Handwritten Notes: Best Practices

Choose clean, professional stationery in neutral tones. Avoid bold patterns or heavily branded designs that can distract from your message. Personalized stationery with your first and last name printed at the top is best. If that's not available, a simple, high-quality "Thank You" notecard works well.

Write with blue or black ink. Keep your handwriting neat, legible, and evenly spaced. The goal is for the reader to focus on your message, not struggle to interpret your writing.

Pro Tip: Whenever possible, hand-deliver your thank-you notes. Drop them at the front desk the next business day and ask the receptionist to pass them along to each interviewer. This personal touch, handwritten and hand-delivered, will set you apart from the other candidates.

From personal experience, this gesture is one of the most impactful ways to leave a lasting impression and set yourself apart. Others are writing thank-you notes, but almost none are hand-delivering them.

Here's an actual response I received after hand-delivering thank-you notes the day after an in-person interview, showing that this small action really does make you stand out:

Hi Lindsay,

I enjoyed speaking with you. Thank you for the note – impressive personal touch and it's much appreciated!

Look forward to speaking with you soon.

If in-person delivery isn't an option, mail your notes promptly, addressing each envelope to the individual interviewer.

If you're mailing the note, use this address format as an example:
XYZ Business
Attn: Name of individual
Address

What to Say

Begin your note with something that shows reflection, enthusiasm, or a personal connection from the conversation.

Examples:

- "Our conversation left me feeling energized by your team's mission and culture."
- "Your description of the internship onboarding process stood out to me and helped me see where I could add value immediately."

What to Include

1. *Open with a connection or reflection.*

   Lead with how the conversation made you feel, what stood out, or what you appreciated.

2. *Express appreciation.*

   Thank them genuinely for their time, insights, or advice.

3. *Mention something specific.*

   Refer to a detail from the conversation (a project, value, or team dynamic) to show you were actively listening.

4. *Reaffirm your interest.*

   Reinforce your enthusiasm for the role and briefly restate how you could add value.

5. *Close with warmth and professionalism.*

   End on a forward-looking note that invites continued connection.

Sample Thank-You Note Template

Dear [Interviewer's Name],

Thank you again for taking the time to speak with me about the [Position Title] role at [Company Name]. Our conversation gave me valuable insight into the position, and I especially appreciated your perspective on how the team is approaching [specific project or goal].

I also found your thoughts on [another specific topic] particularly helpful, as they gave me a clearer picture of the company's values and the kind of meaningful impact this role can have.

Our discussion further confirmed my strong interest in joining [Company or Team Name], and I am excited about the opportunity to contribute my skills and energy to the team's success. Please let me know if there's any additional information I can provide to support your decision-making process.

Thanks again for your time and consideration.

Best regards,
[Your Full Name]
[Your Contact Info, if needed]

Pro Tips

- Even if the interview felt awkward or difficult, send a thank-you note anyway.
- Proofread before sending. Spelling errors or an awkward tone can undercut your message.
- The longer you wait to send a thank-you note, the less appreciation and interest it shows.

Follow Up:
Always follow up if you have not heard back within the expected timeline. This applies to recruiters and hiring managers during the job search, but also to coworkers and customers during an internship. Proactive follow-up shows initiative, accountability, and genuine interest.

Below is a real-life example of when I followed up after a final round interview, as I had not heard back within the timeline outlined. It was well received and initiated a quick response from the hiring manager. Although following up can sometimes make you feel like you're being annoying, as long as it's past the timeline they've outlined, it's absolutely appropriate and usually appreciated.

to me

Hi Lindsay,

First, thank you for your note...

Second, you made a great impression with the team and I...

We are going to sync on Monday as a group when I am back in office and I'll be in touch...

As mentioned, you are one of two finalists and I intend to make a decision Monday.

***

Lindsay
to

Hi

I completely understand and respect taking the time to ensure you make the right hire, but just wanted to follow-up to see if you had any updates.

Thanks in advance!

***

to me

Hi Lindsay,

Apologies for just responding now...
Would love to connect if you have a few minutes now...
I am going to try your cell.

Wrap-Up: The Unspoken Expectations of Interviews

Being prepared means more than following the rules. It means knowing what's expected even when no one spells it out.

Focus on Day-Of Logistics

- **Rule:** Show up on time.
- **Expectation:** Arrive prepared and ready to make a great first impression from the moment you walk in.

Be Prepared

- **Rule:** Answer the questions with answers showing relevant experience.
- **Expectation:** Tell stories that connect your skills to the company's needs, while showing energy and presence.

Look the Part

- **Rule:** Dress appropriately.
- **Expectation:** Your appearance should show respect, attention to detail, and alignment with company culture.

Your Introduction

- **Rule:** Shake hands and smile.
- **Expectation:** Your body language, handshake, and tone should project confidence, trust, and genuine interest.

Follow-Up

- **Rule:** Say "thank you."
- **Expectation:** Follow up quickly with personalized notes to all interviewers that reinforce your interest and appreciation.

Final Takeaway

Getting the interview means your résumé was strong. Getting the offer comes down to presence, preparation, and follow-up. It's not always the smartest candidates who get hired; it's the most prepared. Remember: people want to hire people who show they actually want the opportunity and clearly demonstrate how they can add value. They want to hire people who make them confidently answer yes to these unspoken questions:

- *Can I see myself working with this person every day?*
- *Will they earn the trust and respect of the team?*
- *Would they represent our company well?*

The Unspoken Expectations of How to Earn the Return Offer: From "Summer Help" to "Full-Time Hire"

Once you've landed an internship, it's up to you to maximize the opportunity and position yourself for a full-time return offer. It's important to remember that every action (or inaction) will be noticed and assessed, whether you're in the office or representing the company at events. By the time an internship begins, every intern is qualified. From that point on, success isn't just about working hard or doing the job well; it's about understanding the behaviors and patterns hiring managers consistently observe as they decide who feels ready for a full-time offer.

Internships are the clearest path to proving you're ready for a full-time role, and they are one of the most reliable ways to land a job before graduation. While securing an offer is a huge advantage, your internship is also about learning, gaining experience, building your network, and enjoying the opportunity.

Receiving and Responding to Feedback: How to Use It to Your Advantage

Feedback is part of growth. Many young professionals are never taught how to take it well, so it's an opportunity for you to stand out.

Ask for Feedback

You don't need to wait for formal reviews to get feedback. One of the best habits you can build as an intern is learning how to ask for feedback early and often. The way you request feedback can shape how your manager views you: proactive, self-aware, and ready to learn.

Set Up a Consistent Feedback Loop

If your manager doesn't automatically schedule weekly 1:1s, ask for them. Say something like:

> *"Would you be open to a 15-minute check-in each week so I can stay aligned and keep improving?"*

If schedules don't allow for meetings, propose a quick weekly email exchange where you send a summary of what you worked on and ask for any relevant feedback.

Structure Smart Questions That Invite Real Feedback

Don't just ask, "Do you have any feedback?" Instead, use open-ended questions that invite specifics and show initiative:

- "Is there anything I could've handled differently on that [project/email/presentation]?"
- "What's the team's top priority right now, and how can I help move it forward?"
- "Is there anything I can take off your plate or someone else's?"

These questions shift the dynamic from passively waiting to actively learning.

Ask for Expectations Up Front

Another way to open the door to feedback is to clarify expectations from day one. Try this:

> *"As I get started, I'd love to know what success looks like for this role and how I can best support the team."*

Not only does this help you understand what matters most, but it also makes any future feedback easier to interpret because you'll know what you're being measured against.

Pro Tips:

- *Take Notes*: Write down feedback during or right after your check-in. It shows respect and helps you act on it.

- *Show Progress*: Managers love seeing growth. Reference past feedback and how you've responded to it. This reinforces that you're coachable.

- *Add Value Early and Often*: Asking for feedback isn't just about improving; it's how you confirm you're making a real impact. Don't wait until the final week to find out if you were helpful. Check in regularly to ask, "Am I meeting expectations?" and "Where could I be more useful?" Being a consistent value-add from the start positions you as someone worth keeping.

Bottom Line:

Asking for feedback is important. It shows that you take initiative, value improvement, and want to be an asset. Most interns *don't* do this. So when you do, you instantly set yourself apart.

How to Handle Feedback Professionally

Getting feedback can be uncomfortable, but it's also one of the fastest ways to grow and stand out. Here's how to make sure you handle it like someone ready for more responsibility.

1. Stay Open

What to do:

Before the conversation, remind yourself: *This is meant to help me.*

Even critical feedback means someone believes you're worth coaching.

Pro Tip: Quiet the voice in your head that wants to justify or explain. Focus on receiving, not reacting.

2. Listen Without Defensiveness

What to do:

Let the person finish their thoughts without interrupting, even if you disagree. Keep your body language open: no crossed arms, no fidgeting, no looking at the floor or your phone.

Examples:

- Hold steady eye contact.
- Take slow, quiet breaths to stay grounded.
- Nod occasionally to signal engagement.
- Remind yourself: *This feedback is insight. If I apply it, I increase my chances of earning a return offer.*

Pro Tip: If you tend to get flustered, jot down a few key words during the conversation. It gives you something to focus on and helps you respond thoughtfully.

3. Show You're Engaged

What to do:

Demonstrate that you're paying attention and value the feedback.

Examples:

- Nod subtly while listening.
- Jot down specific suggestions.
- If you're on video, look into the camera, not down or away.
- Be aware of your body language. Even if you're feeling mad, sad, or embarrassed, you don't want others to see that.

4. Ask Clarifying Questions

What to do:

If you don't fully understand the feedback, ask a respectful follow-up question to ensure you're clear on what to work on.

Use these phrases:

- "Can you give me an example of what that looked like?"
- "What would a stronger version have looked like?"
- "If I focused on just one thing this week, what should it be?"
- "Is this something I've done more than once, or was it just in this situation?"

5. Say Thank You

What to do:

Even if the feedback is hard to hear, end with appreciation. It shows emotional maturity.

Say things like:

- "Thanks for the honest feedback. I appreciate you taking the time to help me out."
- "That gives me something concrete to work on. Thank you."
- "This is helpful. I'll start applying it right away."

6. Apply + Follow Up

What to do:

Feedback only matters if you act on it. Make the change, then check back in.

Follow up with:

- "I've been working on [insert feedback]. Can you please let me know if you've seen improvement?"
- "Last week, you mentioned [X]. I tried doing [Y] instead. Is that more in line with what you were expecting?"

What If You Don't Agree With the Feedback?

Not all feedback will feel fair or accurate. That's normal. But how you handle it still says a lot about your professionalism.

What to do: Don't argue. Ask questions and share your perspective calmly.

Use "I" statements like:

- "I interpreted the instructions differently. Can I walk you through how I approached it?"

- "I see your point. Would it help if I explained my thought process?"
- "I wasn't aware of that expectation, but I appreciate the heads-up."

Ask for Clarity Without Sounding Defensive

What to do: Clarify the feedback respectfully, especially if it was vague or unexpected.

Ask questions like:

- "Could you clarify what you meant by [X]?"
- "Are you suggesting I do [Y] differently next time?"
- "What would a more effective version of that look like in your eyes?"

Coachability = Competitive Advantage

Being open to feedback shows:

- Maturity
- Self-awareness
- A growth mindset

People don't expect perfection. They remember how you respond, recover, and improve.

Time and Task Management: How to Be Dependable

Why It Matters

Showing up on time, hitting deadlines, and taking ownership builds trust, and trust leads to more responsibility, return job offers, and promotions.

1. Show Up On Time and Don't Leave Early

What It Looks Like

- In school: "On time" means arriving when it starts.
- In the workplace: "On time" means ready to go *before* it starts.

Why It Matters

Being early shows respect, preparation, and professionalism.

Tips

- Log into virtual meetings a few minutes early.
- Plan ahead for traffic, login issues, or delays.
- Don't leave work early, unless you have a valid reason.
- If you need to stay late for a meeting or to finish a task, do it.

2. Plan for Deadlines

What It Looks Like

- In school: Deadlines are assigned.
- At work: Deadlines aren't always clear, so it's your responsibility to get clarity.

Why It Matters

Understanding expectations and managing time well earns trust and respect.

Tips

- Use a planner or task manager to track deliverables.
- Break large tasks into smaller, timed milestones.

- Clarify timelines with your manager or teammates.
- If someone says "soon," assume they mean ASAP.

3. Use Lunch Breaks Appropriately

Clarify Expectations Early

- Ask on Day 1 (or be observant): "What's the norm around lunch breaks here?"
  - Some offices take a strict 30 or 60 minutes.
  - Others are flexible as long as work gets done.
- Your manager will appreciate that you asked because it shows self-awareness and professionalism.

Stick to the Allotted Time

- If the norm is a one-hour lunch, aim for 50 to 55 minutes.
- If you're running late back to the office, send a quick heads-up. Being consistently late can come off as disrespectful or careless.

Know Where to Eat

- Observe the culture: Do employees eat at their desks? In a lunchroom? Go out together?
- If invited to join a group lunch, go. It's part of maximizing your internship experience by networking and building connections.

Watch Your Behavior During Lunch

- Don't overshare or gossip. Lunch is still part of the workday.

- If you're eating with colleagues or leadership, be mindful of what you say and how you present yourself.
- Put your phone away unless others are using theirs.

Don't Disappear

- Avoid going out for lunch and returning with shopping bags, a new haircut, or personal errands that signal a lack of focus.
- Interns are watched more closely and, unfair or not, how you spend your break reflects your overall professionalism.

During Remote Internships

- Still ask: "What's the typical lunchtime window?"
- Block off lunch on your calendar if appropriate, and communicate if stepping away.
- Be camera-ready when meetings are near your lunch hour (don't show up mid-bite).

4. Stand Out as an Intern Through Task Management

Interns who stay organized and proactive are more likely to earn trust, visibility, and return offers.

Tips

- **Have open communication about deadlines.**

  Communicate early if you hit roadblocks and never wait until the last minute.

  "Just wanted to flag that I may need an extra day. I'm working through [X] but should have it by [new date]."

- **If you finish early, ask what's next.**

  Managers notice initiative.

  "I wrapped that up ahead of schedule. Let me know if there's something else I can support."

- **Use a calendar to organize your day.**

  Block out time for each task and meeting, even if your schedule is flexible.

- **Track your own to-do list.**

  If a manager says, "Let's reconnect next week," be the one to follow up and get it scheduled.

  "Circling back on our last conversation. I wanted to check in and see if now's a good time to revisit [project/topic]."

Meetings and Collaboration Skills: Know When to Speak, Lead, or Listen

How you show up in meetings shapes how colleagues and clients see you. Coming prepared, staying engaged, and showing respect for others' time and input go a long way. Remember, the purpose of a meeting is to move the group forward. Anything that distracts from that, whether it's eating, interrupting, or tuning out, undermines both your contribution and how others perceive you.

In-Person Meetings

- Meeting preparation should include knowing the reason for the meeting and why you're attending, reviewing the agenda items, and preparing something valuable to contribute if appropriate.

- Be aware that you are always a direct reflection of the company/organization you represent.
- Being late is disrespectful. Focus on the time you need to leave for the meeting, not the actual meeting time. Allow yourself an extra 5 to 10 minutes for possible delays. If you are going to be late, give notice so others aren't waiting on you to begin.
- Bring either your laptop or a notebook/pen to take notes.
- If you're hosting a meeting, have a plan for how to deal with potential technology problems and arrive early to help troubleshoot any set-up problems.
- Jot down the names of people present at the meeting and address them by name.
- Be appropriately dressed.
- Be organized and have items such as a pen easily accessible, so you don't have to rummage through your briefcase or purse to find them.
- Be proactive by telling the meeting organizer in advance if you must leave the meeting early.
- Be considerate by silencing your cell phone and keeping it out of sight.
- Be aware of your body language throughout the meeting.
- In a small meeting, if you are offered the choice of the chair either across the table/desk or at an angle from the host, select the angled one. This eliminates the barrier of the table/desk between you, which allows for a more personal connection.
- Be courteous by not interrupting others or dominating the conversation.

- Be gracious by cleaning up after yourself.
- Do not eat in meetings unless it is a working lunch meeting.

Virtual Meetings

- If you're the host, make sure to include the proper link/dial-in information for the meeting on the calendar invite.
- Use a clean, clutter-free background or a virtual background that is subtle and appropriate for the meeting without distracting surroundings. If you're working in a shared space, use the background blur feature to minimize distractions.
- If the host has their camera on, you should also have yours on, especially if it's a small group. If it's a very large meeting or webinar, or if you're joining from an area with bad service, cameras can stay off as long as you are actively staying engaged.
- Ensure your face is well-lit and positioned at eye level with the camera to appear professional.
- Dress as you would for an in-person meeting, especially for client meetings or interviews.
- Be fully dressed appropriately, not just from the waist up, as unexpected events (e.g., standing up) can happen.
- Join a few minutes early to address any last-minute technical issues. Have a backup plan, like dialing in via phone or switching to a secondary device if connection issues arise. If you are hosting, log in at least 5 to 10 minutes early to ensure everything is set up, including screen sharing and presentation tools.

- When entering your name to join a meeting, use this format: Sam Green | Student—University of Wisconsin or Sam Green | Intern.

- Keep your microphone muted when you are not speaking to avoid background noise or interruptions. Be ready to unmute quickly when it is your turn to speak to maintain fluid conversation.

- Make an effort to participate by nodding, reacting, or using chat features to show that you are engaged. Avoid multitasking or looking distracted, as it can be perceived as disrespectful. Turn off computer and phone notifications to prevent distractions during the meeting.

- Wait for pauses to speak and use features like the "raise hand" button when necessary. Overlapping speech can be disruptive.

- Keep chat messages on-topic and professional. Avoid side conversations.

- Good posture conveys professionalism and engagement.

- No eating or chewing gum while on camera.

- End meetings with a courteous goodbye or summary, and allow time for questions or last comments.

- Send meeting notes or action items via email shortly after the meeting to ensure clarity and accountability.

- Always ask for consent before recording a meeting, as privacy remains a priority.

Business Dining Tips: Because You're Always Being Observed

Sooner or later, you will find yourself dining with colleagues—whether it's during an interview, meeting, or an after-hours social gathering. It's important to know how to properly conduct yourself in this type of environment.

Before the Meal

- Know the restaurant and have the host's phone number in case you're running late.
- Arrive five minutes early and dressed appropriately.
- Preview the menu to get an idea of the options that are mid-priced and easy to eat.

During the Meal

- Once everyone is seated, place the napkin on your lap.
- Wait for everyone's food before starting.
- Let the host begin eating first.
- Choose easy-to-eat food.
- Order mid-priced menu items (you don't want to be the one to order the cheapest option, but you also definitely don't want to be the one who orders the most expensive one).
- Be polite to the server. How you treat them is a direct reflection of the way you treat others.
- Don't spend forever choosing your meal because it reflects on your decision-making skills.
- Don't place phones, keys, or bags on the table.

- Focus on conversation and rapport, not the food.

- Take small bites of food and never begin speaking while food remains in your mouth. Gesture by raising your index finger to convey "Just a minute, please."

- Keep pace with others and don't eat too fast or too slow. (Don't be done eating long before anyone else, and don't make people wait long for you to finish.)

- If you need to step away from the table, say, "Excuse me."

At the End

- During an interview, you are a guest. Therefore, when the bill is being signed by the interviewer, say, "Thank you," and say it again when leaving the venue.

- At meal outings during your internship, always offer to pay your portion unless it's a specified work-sponsored event.

Basic Dining Tips

Napkins

- Once everyone is seated, place the napkin on your lap. If everyone else is seated, place your napkin as soon as you take your seat.

- If you leave the table mid-meal, place the napkin on your chair.

- At the end, return it loosely folded to the table.

Silverware

- Use utensils from the outside in. The utensils farthest from your plate are for the first courses (like a salad fork or soup spoon). As the meal progresses, you move inward toward the plate, using the next set of utensils for each new course. The fork and knife closest to your plate are for the main course. If there are utensils above your plate, they are meant for dessert.

- Never wave silverware when speaking.
- Use your dinner fork (not the salad fork) if salad is the main course.

Glasses & Plates

- Bread plate = upper left; drink = upper right (tip: left-hand "b" for bread, right-hand "d" for drink).
- If someone takes your bread plate or glass, don't call it out; just adapt or ask the server for a new one if necessary.

Soup

- Scoop soup away from you and sip from the side of the spoon.
- Don't blow on hot soup or dunk bread.
- When finished, place the spoon on the saucer (or in the bowl if there isn't one).

Bread

- Tear rolls, don't cut them.
- Place butter on your bread plate before spreading.
- Don't drag the bread plate closer to you.
- If using shared olive oil, spoon some onto your plate and don't double-dip.

Miscellaneous

- Don't start eating until everyone is served.
- When you need an item that is out of your reach, say, "Please pass the [item]."
- Pass items (food, salt and pepper) to your right unless the person who is making the request is seated next to you on your left.
- Don't season your food before tasting it.
- Use your hand as a shield when squeezing lemon.
- Cut no more than one or two bites of meat at a time, as this keeps the uncut portion warm and also helps prevent you from eating too fast.
- Don't chew ice.
- Don't bring leftovers home from an interview or business meal.
- Bring small bills for valet, coat check, etc.

Ownership and Accountability: Act Like an Employee When You're "Just an Intern"

Taking initiative means stepping up without being asked. It's one of the clearest signs of leadership potential, even at the intern level. The more consistently you add value, the more others will see you as essential, not optional. Here are some examples of how you can show initiative:

- Volunteer to take notes.
- Send a meeting recap.
- Say, "I've got it" when something needs to be done.

- Ask, "What else can I help with?" or "Is there anything I can take off your plate?"

Learning from Mistakes

If you make a mistake, **don't:**

- Hide it
- Make excuses
- Lie

Do:

- Own it early: "I missed the mark, but here's what I'm doing to fix it."
- Share the plan: "I underestimated the time, so I've adjusted my approach moving forward."
- Follow through on your fix.
- Don't ghost, deflect, or hide the mistake.

Example:

"I forgot to send the meeting invite by mistake. I sent an email to the attendees apologizing for my mistake and confirming that the proposed time still works for them. Moving forward, I will make sure to send an invite as soon as a date and time are identified so it doesn't happen again."

Be a Low-Maintenance, High-Impact Intern

Be the person who makes your manager's life easier, not harder. The interns who show initiative, communicate clearly, and follow through without needing constant reminders earn more trust, responsibility, and return offers. This is the type of person others like working with.

- **Be Proactive with Updates**

  Don't wait to be asked what you're working on. Send brief, regular updates (daily or weekly, depending on the pace of your role). Even a short message like:

  "Finished [X], starting [Y], will have a draft by [Z]. Let me know if priorities shift," shows maturity and initiative.

- **Create a Weekly Summary**

  At the end of each week, send a short recap:

  - What you accomplished
  - What's still in progress
  - Any challenges or issues where help is needed
  - What you're working on next

  This simple habit signals ownership and gives your manager clarity without needing to check in constantly.

- **Clarify Expectations Up Front**

  Don't assume you know what "ASAP" or "done" means. Ask:

  - "When would you like this finished?"
  - "What's the format or level of detail you're expecting?"
  - "Who should I loop in before sending this out?"

- **Avoid Asking the Same Question Twice**

  Take notes. Reference them before repeating a question. It's okay to ask for help, but it's not okay to appear careless or disorganized.

- **Try First, Then Ask with Context**

  Before asking for help, show what you tried and where you got stuck:

  "I reviewed the onboarding doc and tried [X] and [Y], but I'm still stuck on [Z]. My guess is it might be related to [_____]. Can you point me in the right direction?" This shows you're putting in effort, not just asking for the answer.

- **Respect Your Manager's Time**

  Your manager or mentor is juggling multiple responsibilities. Don't interrupt them with every question. Instead, batch your questions and keep messages concise. Respect their calendar and prepare for meetings ahead of time.

  Example:

  "Just a quick update: I finished [X], am starting on [Y], and I've blocked time to review [Z] by Friday. Let me know if I should shift priorities."

- **Observe Others in Positions Above You**

  When you start mirroring people in higher roles, people naturally start picturing you at the next level.

  - Observe how the stand-out full-time entry-level employees work.

  - How do they write emails? Handle feedback? Speak in meetings?

  - Emulate their tone, work habits, and professionalism.

  - Dress for the job you want, not the job you have.

- **Look for What's Missing**

  Every team has blind spots, busywork, or small pain points. If you notice something you can improve, even if it's small, speak up or offer to help.

  Examples:

  ○ "I noticed the client folder is unorganized. I can help organize it to make it easier to use."

  ○ "I created a checklist to streamline [task] since I kept having to double-check myself. Happy to share it if it's useful for others."

- **Keep a "Wins + Lessons" Document**

  Throughout your internship, track:

  ○ Small wins and contributions

  ○ Praise or feedback you receive

  ○ Mistakes and what you learned

  This becomes your go-to for:

  ○ Midpoint check-ins

  ○ Final reviews

  ○ Updating your résumé

  ○ Asking for a return offer

Actions that Speak Louder than Words: How to Add Value

1. **Respect People's Time**

   ○ Be on time to meetings, deadlines, and calls.

   ○ Don't waste others' time by rambling or showing up unprepared.

- ○ Batch questions or requests when possible and avoid constant pings.
- ○ Find ways to make your manager's life easier (and to make them look good to their managers).
- ○ Make sure you check people's availability before scheduling meetings. Oftentimes, you'll have access to view your coworkers' calendars.

2. **Respect Communication Norms**
   - ○ Use clear, professional language, especially in writing.
   - ○ Avoid typing in all caps, using slang, or overusing exclamation points.
   - ○ Don't CC senior leaders unnecessarily or jump the chain of command.
   - ○ Keep emails and messages short, clear, and purposeful.
   - ○ Respect the preferred communication channel. For example, if employees use an internal tool like Slack, respect that and don't text your coworkers even if that's what you prefer.
   - ○ Learn the language of the business, which is often filled with acronyms and terms that are specific to the business/role/industry. Listen and make an effort to use them.

3. **Respect Workspaces**
   - ○ In person: Keep noise down (music, your voice, ringtones, etc.), avoid interrupting, honor physical boundaries, and clean up after yourself.
   - ○ Remote: Stay on mute when not speaking and use video respectfully (no eating on camera and dress appropriately).

4. Respect Boundaries

- Don't ask details about coworkers' personal lives unless they bring it up. Asking one to two questions to show interest is great, but if they aren't providing much information, don't push.
- Keep jokes workplace-appropriate, and if you're not sure, don't say it.
- Not everyone wants to connect outside of work, and that's okay.

5. Respect Cultural & Generational Differences

- Be mindful of varying work styles and communication preferences.
- Observe first, adapt second.
- Ask when unsure instead of making assumptions.

6. Respect the Work Itself

- Review your work before submitting. Sloppy work shows a lack of care.
- Don't change shared documents without asking first.
- Acknowledge others' contributions and give credit where it's due.

7. Respect Feedback

- Receive it with gratitude, not defensiveness.
- Show you've applied it. Follow up later with:

"I incorporated your suggestion. Does this version feel stronger?"

8. **Respect the Opportunity**
   - Say thank you often, and actually mean it.
   - Take initiative without waiting to be told.
   - Be prepared, stay curious, stay coachable, and stay engaged.

Other In-Office Tips to Consider

- Stay off your cell phone (especially social media) during work hours. Make sure notifications are silenced.

- Always resist answering a question or commenting on a conversation that you overhear in the cubicle next to you.

- Behave as though cubicles have doors. Lightly knock or announce yourself at the entrance.

- If someone is on the phone, come back when they are finished. Do not hover until they hang up.

- Pay attention to the volume of your voice while speaking on the phone or to other colleagues.

- Use headphones for listening to music or any audio content to avoid disturbing others.

- In a cubicle arrangement, remember that food odors, especially from hot food, can bother your neighbors.

- Perfumes and heavily scented hand lotions should be avoided.

- Be conscientious with personal or sensitive calls or conversations; assume that your colleagues can hear your end of the conversation.

- If working in a shared space, use backgrounds for video calls that are clean and professional, and be considerate of what might be visible to others. For example, don't have other people in your background who might not know they're on camera.

- Clean up after yourself in shared spaces, such as kitchens, lounges, and conference rooms. Leave them as you found them or better.

- Use the office's room-booking system for meetings and respect reservation times.

- When using the fridge, label your food, don't leave items past their expiration date, and avoid storing strong-smelling meals.

- Do not eat other people's food or drink other people's beverages that are in the shared office fridge.

- Know your company's lunch culture and policies. Avoid consistently taking breaks that are longer than the norm. If you're leaving the office, let your team know.

- Do not make calls in the office bathroom.

- Do not approach a coworker with questions or concerns as soon as they arrive at work. Give them a moment to get settled.

- Use greetings like "hello" or "good morning" with your coworkers, even if you don't know them well.

Show You Want the Return Offer: How to Leave the Best Last Impression After an Internship

- Write handwritten thank-you notes for everyone who impacted your internship.
  - Make them personalized—mention a specific time that was memorable.
  - Hand deliver them on your last day.
  - Yes, this can be time-consuming, but this is one of the most effective ways to put yourself in a strong position for a return offer.
  - Personalized stationery with your first and last name on it is more expensive than generic thank-you note cards, but I highly recommend investing in it.

Here are a few reactions to handwritten thank-you notes my husband delivered on the last day of his internship:

Subject: Thank You Note

Dylan,

Got your thank you note when I was back in the office and wanted to return the thank you. Was great working with you and hope to see you around again in the future. All the best and great work throughout. Class act sharing a hand-written note.

Subject: Congrats!

Dylan — congratulations on the full time offer! That is great news and very well deserved! As you are thinking through the offer, please let me know if I can be helpful in any way. Also, thank you for the very kind hand written note on your last day!

Wrap-Up: The Unspoken Expectations of How to Earn the Return Offer

Being prepared means more than following the rules. It means knowing what's expected even when no one spells it out.

Be Coachable

- **Rule:** Listen to your manager and coworkers.
- **Expectation:** Ask for feedback early, apply it, and circle back to show growth.

Be Dependible

- **Rule:** Show up and meet deadlines.
- **Expectation:** Anticipate priorities, respect your manager's time, and deliver early when possible.

Add Value

- **Rule:** Attend meetings on time and listen.
- **Expectation:** Come prepared, engage respectfully, and add value to the conversation.

Be Likeable

- **Rule:** Be polite and kind.
- **Expectation:** Respect norms, boundaries, and cultures in ways that make you easy and enjoyable to work with. Leave people wanting to work with you again by saying thank you, showing professionalism, and being kind.

Final Takeaway

Earning a return offer isn't guaranteed. You need to show that you're already thinking and acting like a future full-time hire. Remember: people want to work with those they like, who add value, and who are reliable.

Conclusion

By now, you've seen that landing an internship and turning it into a full-time return offer is about far more than qualifications. It is about preparation: knowing how to demonstrate to employers that you are someone they want on their team, who represents the company well, and who quickly earns the trust and respect of colleagues.

Most students dismiss these skills as "common sense." You now know better. These are learned skills, and they are your competitive advantage. From this point forward, you'll start to notice others falling short without even realizing it, while you'll pursue opportunities with confidence from knowing exactly what to do, when to do it, and how to do it.

To make it simple, I've included a quick Unspoken Expectations Cheatsheet below. This is a recap of some of the most important lessons to keep top of mind.

Your Unspoken Expectations Cheatsheet

The quickest way ...

- *To build initial trust and rapport*—maintain eye contact during an introduction and handshake
- *To show your confidence*—good posture

- *To start a conversation*—ask an open-ended question (how, what, why) or give a compliment
- *To ruin a first impression*—avoid eye contact
- *To enhance your professional presence*—understand the importance of business attire and attention to details
- *To sound more professional on the telephone*—use the person's name
- *To prevent sending an email message before you are ready*—draft and proofread your message before you type in the recipient's email address
- *To remember someone's name*—say it quickly in your head and then use it
- *To be on time*—focus on the time you need to leave for the interview or meeting, not the start time
- *To get others to treat you with respect*—respect others by always being polite

Your Next Step

You don't need years of experience to act like a professional.

Many young professionals miss out on internship opportunities not because they lack talent, but because no one ever taught them the unspoken expectations of the workplace. They don't know what they don't know. As a result, they continue to make small mistakes that cost them opportunities without even realizing why.

But you're no longer in the dark. You can now show up more confidently because you know what to expect and what's expected of you.

Starting tomorrow, choose one expectation from this book and put it into practice. Over time, the small, consistent actions will help build a reputation of trust, reliability, and professionalism—the qualities that actually get people internships, full-time offers, and promotions.

Being *The Prepared Intern* is what will set you apart.

About the Authors

Lindsay Muench

Lindsay Muench spent over a decade in corporate America at companies such as Oracle, HubSpot, and The Mom Project. From the start of her career, she noticed something that stuck with her: opportunities didn't always go to the smartest or most experienced candidates; they went to the ones who were the most prepared.

She had a built-in advantage. Her mom was a business etiquette trainer, so Lindsay grew up learning how much presence, connection, confidence, and thoughtful follow-up matter in every interaction. Later, she realized those "common-sense" skills weren't common at all; they were a competitive advantage.

Lindsay never had intentions to write a book. But that changed after she saw the positive impact these "common sense" skills had when her husband needed to quickly transition from being a fighter pilot in the military to a civilian working in corporate America.

With no prior business background, he pursued a career in investment banking. Instead of focusing on his résumé and how to justify his lack of relevant experience, Lindsay helped him learn what employers want and expect, but don't actually list on job descriptions. The stuff that can quickly elevate a candidate with basic qualifications or, just as quickly, sink someone highly qualified. He landed the internship and then received a full-time return offer. Witnessing his successful transition inspired her to help those at the beginning of their careers put their best selves forward from the start.

Today, Lindsay is on a mission to help students understand that landing internship opportunities isn't just about having good grades or an impressive résumé; it's also about being prepared to meet and exceed the expectations employers *actually* have. She's the Founder of *The Prepared Intern*, which helps students start their senior year with a job offer in hand by focusing on what matters beyond how qualified they are on paper.

Lindsay graduated from Elon University with a Bachelor of Science in Business Administration, with a focus on Marketing and Sales. She lives in Richmond, Virginia, with her husband, their two children, and their golden retriever.

Susan Richardson

Susan Richardson founded Etiquette Essentials LLC in 1995, delivering national business etiquette seminars to clients that included numerous Fortune 500 companies, small businesses, and universities. She retired in 2019.

For more content and resources, follow @thepreparedintern on Instagram.